DEAR FELLOW MEMBER:
The basic unit of society is the family. It's where
we receive our training and the direction for our
lives. As family members, we also have a distinct sense of belonging.

In The Family, by Associate Teacher Paul Van
Gorder, tells you what it means to belong to the
family of God. These lessons from First John
will help you understand your responsibilities
to the Lord and to your brothers and sisters in
Christ. They will bring you encouragement,
instruction, and hope.

Please accept this book as a gift from the Radio
Bible Class. It's our way of saying "THANK
YOU" for all you've done for us in the past
year. It has been a year of growth, and it would
have been impossible without your prayers and
support.

So, again, thank you, and may God richly bless
you.

Richard W. DeHaan

Teacher, RADIO BIBLE CLASS

IN THE FAMILY

FAMILY

Lessons from First John

by Paul R. Van Gorder

IN THE FAMILY

PREFACE

The first epistle of John has often been called the letter of fellowship—a family fellowship made possible by a vital, living relationship with God in Jesus Christ.

I do not attempt nor pretend a complete exposition of this charming epistle. Rather I have set forth the dominant themes presented by John that relate to the "family circle"—the "little born ones" in the household of faith. Amazingly, the truths essential to the "bairns" are also applicable and appropriate for those children who have long been in the family. All believers, therefore, can benefit from a fresh study of John's first epistle. May our Lord be pleased to use this repetition of His Word to the training and maturing of all His children.

This is a letter of light, love, and life. It speaks to the vital questions of Christian fellowship, both vertical (between Father and child) and horizontal (within the circle of saints). As its message is understood and applied, it can only draw us closer to our Heavenly Father and to one another as believers in Christ.

Paul Van Gorder

CONTENTS

INTRODUCTION

Few words take on greater significance to a child than those contained in a letter from his father. The apostle John repeatedly referred to the Christians he was writing as "my little children." This is the basis of the fellowship that is at the heart of his epistle—a fellowship made possible through a family relationship.

In his *gospel*, John had presented Jesus Christ as God's Son "made flesh and dwelt among us." Christ is the life—eternal life. He gave Himself for us, laying down His own life and then rising again so that we might live. He secured this same life for all who believe on Him.

In John's first *epistle*, the characteristics of eternal life possessed by every believer in Christ are set forth. That eternal life in us must be the same as in Him. *Like* must go with *like*.

Probably written from Ephesus in the latter years of John's life, perhaps just prior to his imprisonment on Patmos, this epistle may be the last apostolic message to the entire church. John's second and third epistles, you will remember, were addressed to individuals.

C. I. Scofield wrote, "The *gospel* [of John] shows us the Father's thoughts and ways with the Son; the *epistle* the Father's thoughts and ways with the sons. The *gospel* leads us across the Father's threshold; the *epistle* makes us at home in the Father's house."

This, then, is the Father's letter to His family. Centering in fellowship, it includes pertinent matters relating to the daily walk, to sin, to attitudes, to brotherly love, and to chastening.

1 John 1:1-4

That which was from the beginning, which we have heard, which we have seen with our eyes, which we have looked upon, and our hands have handled, of the Word of life

(For the life was manifested, and we have seen it, and bear witness, and show unto you that eternal life, which was with the Father, and was manifested unto us)—

That which we have seen and heard declare we unto you, that ye also may have fellowship with us; and truly our fellowship is with the Father, and with His Son, Jesus Christ.

And these things write we unto you, that your joy may be full.

1
Fellowship in the Family

Fellowship with our Heavenly Father begins with a proper view of His Son, the Lord Jesus Christ. Perish the thought that God would ever approve us as sons, or give us opportunity for communion with Him, apart from an understanding of who Christ is and a sincere belief in what He has done! This is the starting point of 1 John.

The Lord Jesus, the eternal, living Word, has become incarnate. In the opening verses of his *gospel*, John wrote, "In Him was life; and the life was the light of men" (John 1:4). Here in his first *epistle*, he immediately focused our attention on Christ the life. This is because three false views of the nature of Christ had sprung up early in the apostolic age. One denied His deity; another denied His humanity; still another denied the union of His two natures. John corrected all three errors in the first two verses of this epistle.

CHRIST'S DEITY (v. 1)

John's very first words are a stirring affirmation

of the deity of Christ. "That which *was from the beginning.* . . ." Charles Ryrie pointed out that the verb "was" means "was already in existence." At that moment in the past when time began, Christ already was. He is eternal, John says, and therefore He is God.

When the prophet Micah predicted the birth of our Lord some seven centuries beforehand, he wrote, "But thou, Bethlehem Ephrathah, though thou be little among the thousands of Judah, yet out of thee shall He come forth unto Me that is to be ruler in Israel, *whose goings forth have been from of old, from everlasting*" (Micah 5:2). Writing by inspiration, the prophet stated that Christ, the one born in Bethlehem as Micah predicted, was without beginning.

John had also attested to the deity of Christ in his gospel. Identifying Him as the Word, he said that like the Heavenly Father, He has always existed.

In the beginning was the Word, and the Word was with God, and the Word was God.

The same was in the beginning with God (John 1:1,2).

The unique personification of wisdom found in Proverbs 8 contains a clear foreshadowing of Christ's eternality, for these verses speak of Him.

The Lord possessed Me in the beginning of His way, before His works of old.

I was set up from everlasting, from the beginning, or ever the earth was.

When there were no depths, I was brought forth—when there were no fountains abounding with water.

Before the mountains were settled, before
the hills, was I brought forth;

While as yet He had not made the earth,
nor the fields, nor the highest part of the
dust of the world.

When He prepared the heavens, I was
there; when He set a compass upon the face
of the depth;

When He established the clouds above;
when He strengthened the fountains of the
deep;

When He gave to the sea its decree, that
the waters should not pass His commandment; when He appointed the foundations
of the earth,

Then I was by Him, as One brought up
with Him; and I was daily His delight, rejoicing always before Him (Proverbs 8:22-
30).

When everything began, Christ always *was*. He
had no beginning. This is the One in whom
eternal life is manifested. This living and lifegiving Word is Jesus Christ. Former ages are
simply the history of man—fallen man. Now the
second man had come. The express image of the
Father, He is the Eternal Word (see Hebrews
1:3). He is the *eternal Son* of the *eternal Father*—
He is God!

The Scriptures teach that Christ was the Son
of God long before He came into the world.
John said that He was "in the bosom of the
Father" (John 1:18). As the eternal Son, He was
before David. He Himself declared that David
had called Him "Lord" (Luke 20:41,42). As the
eternal Son, He was before Moses, for Moses

had esteemed "the reproach of Christ greater riches than the treasures in Egypt" (Hebrews 11:26). As the eternal Son, He was before Abraham, for He said, "Verily, verily, I say unto you, Before Abraham was, I am" (John 8:58). As the eternal Son, He was present and active in creation, for we read that God "created *all things* by Jesus Christ" (Ephesians 3:9). In His prayer to the Father, Christ spoke of Himself as being loved by the Father "before the foundation of the world" (John 17:24).

If you want to know what God is like, look into the face of Jesus Christ. If you want to know how God acts, look at the works of Jesus Christ. He is God's revelation of Himself to man. In essence and character, Christ is the exact image of God. "For it pleased the Father that in Him should all fullness dwell" (Colossians 1:19).

CHRIST'S HUMANITY

When God determined to make His final and complete revelation, when He decided to put into a *word* all the thought of His mind and heart, He bound all up into one great Word, Jesus Christ. He who is the exact image of God's person took upon Himself our humanity and was born as a baby in Bethlehem.

> And the Word was made flesh, and dwelt among us (and we beheld His glory, the glory as of the only begotten of the Father), full of grace and truth (John 1:14).

To establish the human nature of Christ, John called to witness the evidence provided by three senses. They are the test of His humanity. He said first, ". . . we have heard" (1 John 1:1). But someone objects: "John, maybe you *did* hear Him speak. But are you sure it wasn't a distant voice hidden somewhere within His person?"

So the apostle adds, "which we have seen with our eyes." Even that may not be enough, for it could have been only an ephemeral vision, an illusion. But John is not speaking of a fleeting appearance such as that to the two disciples on the road to Emmaus. They knew Him for only a moment, and then He vanished from their sight. John intended far more than that, for he elaborated by saying, ". . . which we have looked upon." A different word is used for "looked upon" than for "see." It means, "to behold with a sense of contemplation; to view attentively, deliberately." John is actually saying, "He was before our eyes so long that we were able to gaze intently upon Him."

Even beyond hearing and seeing is the proof of touch. The One whom the apostle looked upon was no spirit, no phantom, no ghost. John said, "our hands have handled!" To give Thomas the full assurance of who He was, the Lord said, "Handle Me and see." John also saw, touched, and believed.

THE LIFE MANIFESTED IN TIME (v. 2)

John went on to say that "the life was manifested, and we have seen it, and bear witness, and show unto you that eternal life, which was with the Father, and was manifested unto us" (v. 2). Who would dare ask Almighty God to reveal this life to man? The apostle Paul wrote, "There is none that seeketh after God"

(Romans 3:11). Yet God *has* revealed Himself in the person of His Son, for John said in his gospel, "And the Word was made flesh, and dwelt among us (and we beheld His glory . . .)" (John 1:14). Let's look at the phrases of this crucial verse more closely.

"Made Flesh"

God came to us in the person of His Son, "the Word . . . made flesh." Paul said that Christ was "made in the likeness of men" (Philippians 2:7). Think of the distance between the Word and the flesh! It's the distance between infinite and finite, between Creator and created, between Heaven and earth. In the eternal plan of the Godhead, however, it was ordained that the gap should be bridged; that the eternal Word should be revealed as a man.

Most musicians have heard of "sympathetic vibrations." On occasion I have struck a note on the piano, or set a combination of stops on the organ and sounded a chord. From some part of the room I have heard a vibration—perhaps from a window or door, a hanging picture, or a chandelier. That object has picked up the vibration of the organ chord. Friend, not a note can be sounded in our humanity that does not awaken a vibration in the being of Christ. He became man. He knows our every sorrow and temptation. He was "made flesh."

"And Dwelt Among Us"

Not only did God the Son become man, He *"tabernacled* among us." This word turns our thoughts back to the wanderings of the children of Israel in the wilderness. At that time Jehovah dwelt in a tent in the midst of His people. Our

Lord's transient visit to this earth marked the time when the true Tabernacle was here among men, and through that One shone the shekinah glory.

"We Beheld His Glory"

In his epistle, John expands upon his statement in the gospel, "We beheld His glory," by saying, "We have seen with our eyes, . . . we have looked upon." "No mistake," John says, "I saw Him. My eyes may now be dim with the passing years, but these very eyes looked upon Him." The beloved disciple not only saw Him in the day-to-day routine of His earthly ministry, but also in majesty during that memorable night upon Mount Transfiguration. For a brief moment Christ's transcendent glory broke through the veil of His flesh and John "beheld His glory." The poet has written,

> O prodigious wonder,
> To be sounded by the thunder,
> Our God—on earth a child!

The One with us, seen by John and the disciples, was "the light of men." God in Christ, this eternal life which was with the Father, has been revealed unto us. Here is the Light in the midst of a surrounding darkness which did not know Him and could not comprehend Him. Of whom does John speak when he says, "the life was manifested"? None other than the Lord Jesus Christ! He passed from eternity into the limits of time, out of the invisible to the visible. John is decisive! God the Son was really here!

Think of it! The one who wrote these words had "known Christ after the flesh" (2 Corinthians 5:16). John, that beloved disciple, had

leaned upon Jesus' breast. He had felt the beat
of His heart; he had heard His voice of compassion and command; he had seen the glory of
God in the face of Jesus Christ. The One who
was with the Father from all eternity past had
stepped from that illimitable ocean of "forever"
onto the shore of time. God had revealed Himself in the person of His Son.

THE PURPOSE OF THE EPISTLE (v. 3)

The beloved apostle wrote these believers much
in the same vein as when He spoke to the San-
hedrin following the healing of the impotent
man at the gate of the temple. "For we cannot
but speak the things which we have seen and
heard" (Acts 4:20). John's personal, intimate
knowledge of Jesus Christ has been communicated to us. To hear him simply say that he
had "seen and heard" would be of little value to
us. It would be like seeing a photograph or
hearing the transcript of some shorthand
reporting. We would have to align ourselves
with Philip when he said to the Savior, "Lord,
show us the Father, and it sufficeth us" (John
14:8). What pity and rebuke came from the lips
of the Lord Jesus in response! "Have I been
such a long time with you, and yet hast thou
not known Me, Philip? He that hath seen Me
hath seen the Father; and how sayest thou then,
Show us the Father?" (John 14:9). To know
Christ is to know God!

The Holy Spirit who taught John and the
apostles, also teaches us. We therefore understand what eternal life is. Our Lord testified in
His high-priestly prayer for His people, "And

this is life eternal, that they may know Thee, the only true God, *and Jesus Christ*, whom Thou hast sent" (John 17:3).

The apostle John is not the only one to enjoy personal fellowship with God. We too are partners with the Father and His Son Jesus Christ. What higher purpose or occupation could we have! We have fellowship with the Father and with His Son! Consider these words of our Lord to His disciples:

At that day ye shall know that I am in My Father, and ye in Me, and I in you.

He that hath My commandments, and keepeth them, he it is that loveth Me; and he that loveth Me shall be loved of My Father, and I will love him, and will manifest Myself to him.

Judas saith unto Him, not Iscariot, Lord, how is it that Thou wilt manifest Thyself unto us, and not unto the world?

Jesus answered, and said unto him, If a man love Me, he will keep My words; and My Father will love him, and We will come unto him, and make Our abode with him (John 14:20-23).

Amazing fact! Father *and* Son have taken up residence in the believer in the person of the Holy Spirit.

The word "fellowship" is from a Greek word which means, "a relationship between individuals involving a common interest, and a mutual participation in that interest." That God and the believer could have anything in common is almost unfathomable! Yet we have been made partakers of the divine nature. This necessarily means that we will love holiness and hate sin, and we will strive to please Him in all we do.

Our fellowship with the Father and with His Son also makes possible a fellowship with all believers. The apostle John said, "that ye also may have fellowship with us." Paul wrote, "God is faithful, by whom ye were called unto the fellowship of His Son, Jesus Christ our Lord" (1 Corinthians 1:9). You and I as believers have been called into a joint participation with God's Son. This unique relationship is shared by all of God's children. Jesus is the "firstborn among many brethren," and we are "joint heirs with Christ."

JOY! JOY! JOY! (v. 4)
John said he wrote these words in his first epistle so that we might experience full joy. Fellowship always results in happiness. Christ spoke of His joy abiding in us (John 15:11). If you believe what has been declared by the apostles and receive eternal life—that Life who was with the Father and has been manifested to us—then you will have "joy unspeakable and full of glory" (1 Peter 1:8).

John's purpose in this declaration was for our fellowship and joy. No higher blessing on earth could be ours than to commune with the Father and with His Son! This privilege is maintained by our obedience to Christ. The Lord Jesus said,

> If ye keep My commandments, ye shall abide in My love, even as I have kept My Father's commandments, and abide in His love.

These things have I spoken unto you, that My joy might remain in you, and that your joy might be full (John 15:10,11).

Dear friend, here at the beginning of our study of 1 John, I want to ask you several important questions: Do you have fellowship with the Father and with the Son? Do you know that you have eternal life abiding in you? If not, settle these important issues right now. Near the close of the epistle, John wrote,

He that hath the Son hath life; and he that hath not the Son of God hath not life.

These things have I written unto you that believe on the name of the Son of God, that ye may know that ye have eternal life, and that ye may believe on the name of the Son of God (1 John 5:12,13).

Though we may not be able to say, "I heard His voice, I saw Him with my physical eyes, with my hands I have touched Him," we may nevertheless with assurance declare, "I know the Living Christ! His Spirit bears witness with my spirit that I am a child of God."

1 John 1:5-7

This, then, is the message which we have heard of Him, and declare unto you, that God is light, and in Him is no darkness at all.

If we say that we have fellowship with Him, and walk in darkness, we lie, and do not the truth;

But if we walk in the light, as He is in the light, we have fellowship one with another, and the blood of Jesus Christ, His Son, cleanseth us from all sin.

2
Watch Where You Walk!

I heard the voice of Jesus say,
   "I am this dark world's Light;
Look unto Me, thy morn shall rise,
   And all thy day be bright."

I looked to Jesus, and I found
   In Him my Star, my Sun;
And in that Light of life I'll walk,
   Till traveling days are done.

What a privilege to walk hand in hand with
Christ, our light! This chorus of a familiar hymn
expresses the beauty of that relationship:

Friendship with Jesus,
   Fellowship divine,
O what blessed sweet communion!
Jesus is a friend of mine.

Read the refrain of that sweet gospel song once
again. "Fellowship divine!" That's the theme of
John's first epistle. Writing to the family of God,
the apostle had stated his purpose as follows:

". . . that ye also may have fellowship with us; and truly our fellowship is with the Father, and with His Son, Jesus Christ" (1 John 1:3). The highest privilege of a believer in the Lord Jesus is full, unhindered fellowship with the Father.

Being born into God's family is one thing; maintaining fellowship is quite another. Daily living becomes the testing ground of faith. When we disobey our Heavenly Father, our communion with Him is affected.

A child may proclaim with vigor that he bears the family name. He may insist that he is the son of his father. But their communion, the warm atmosphere of fellowship between them, is contingent upon that child's behavior. It is determined by the way he responds to the character of his father. The same is true in the family of God. Our fellowship with our Heavenly Father and with His Son is a fellowship in light, and it rests upon God's very nature.

THE CHARACTER OF THE FATHER (v. 5)
The apostle John began this section by making certain the children in the household of God knew that he was relaying a truth which had come directly from the Lord Jesus Himself. As an apostle, he had heard Him, seen Him, and touched Him. Therefore he wrote, "This, then, is the message which we have heard of Him" (v. 5). What he said about God did not originate from some flash of keen insight, nor from some deduction arrived at through personal observation; rather, it had come as a direct communication from the Lord to His disciples. You and I,

in turn, must accept and rely upon this inspired Word—a Word of revelation to us through the biblical writer.

What had John heard that was so important to the members of God's family? "God is light, and in Him is no darkness at all" (v. 5). This tells us about the character, the very nature of God! How striking that the Holy Spirit told us "God is light" even before He informed us that "God is love" (1 John 4:8).

We are living in an age of permissiveness and moral decay. It may accurately be described by the phrase, "anything goes." It characterizes God as a benevolent grandfather who winks at sin and tolerates the spirit of our time. But according to John, this depiction is totally inaccurate. God is both light and love, and accepting one aspect without the other gives an erroneous conception of His character.

God is absolute in holiness, for "in Him is no darkness at all." Because He is perfect in character, in Him is found no flaw, no darkness, no mistake, no weakness, no easygoing way regarding evil, and no overlooking of the least defiling element. And because Jesus Christ is the revealer of God the Father, He could say, "I am the light of the world" (John 8:12). It would be audacious for Him to make that claim if He were mere man—but how blessed the truth that He is God's Son!

Yes, God is light. James said that God is "the Father of lights, with whom is no variableness, neither shadow of turning" (James 1:17). Then he went on to say that as children of God we have been begotten "with the word of truth, that we should be a kind of firstfruits of His creatures" (James 1:18). Paul the apostle wrote,

For God, who commanded the light to shine out of darkness, hath shone in our hearts, to give the light of the knowledge of the glory of God in the face of Jesus Christ" (2 Corinthians 4:6).

The nature of God—absolute holiness and complete freedom from evil—was manifested in the life of the Lord Jesus. Therefore, to have fellowship with the Father and with the Son is to have fellowship with the light.

Our knowledge of God does not come through rationalistic discovery but through revelation. John said, "This, then, is the message *which we have heard of Him*, and declare unto you, that God is light, and in Him is no darkness at all" (1 John 1:5). The revelation of God as light had begun in the Old Testament. Habakkuk wrote,

And His brightness was like the light. . . .

The sun and moon stood still in their habitation; at the light of Thine arrows they went, and at the shining of Thy glittering spear (Habakkuk 3:4,11).

This One who is the high and unapproachable Light had made Himself known to mankind. How amazing! Of His Son it was said, "In Him was life; and the life was the light of men" (John 1:4). This One who is the Light and the Life came to reveal the Father (John 1:18). As we contemplate all the perfections of Christ—His obedience, His purity, His holiness, and His sinlessness—we must agree with His words to Philip, "He that hath seen Me hath seen the

Father" (John 14:9). Only deity can reveal deity!

A CHRISTIAN OUT OF CHARACTER (v. 6)
Because God is light, the new life He gave us as believers can only have the nature and character of light. When we received Christ, therefore, we were given both *life* and *light*. Paul told the Thessalonian believers, "Ye are all sons of light, and sons of the day; we are not of the night, nor of darkness" (1 Thessalonians 5:5).

The drastic change worked in our lives by the Holy Spirit in the new birth brought with it a new, higher expectation. A new nature, the divine nature, has been implanted in us. Paul wrote, "For ye were once darkness, but now are ye light in the Lord; walk as children of light" (Ephesians 5:8). If indeed we have been brought into the fellowship with God but continue to walk in darkness, "we lie, and do not the truth" (v. 6). The one precludes the other: the new life brings a new manner of living. "For what fellowship hath righteousness with unrighteousness? And what communion hath light with darkness?" (2 Corinthians 6:14). Walking *in* the light and presence of God means fellowship; walking *outside* of it means we're stumbling in Satan's darkness.

The word for "walk" in verse 7 is from a Greek term which means "to go about." It refers to our conduct—our thoughts, words, and deeds. The regular pattern of our lives must be consistent with the light.

Is it possible for one who has been born again to walk in darkness? Someone immediately answers, "Of course not!" Now wait just a moment. The word translated "fellowship" in this epistle is most certainly *not* a synonym for salvation. Having addressed his letter to "my little children," John is speaking to members of God's family. His clearly stated purpose is that these believers may have fellowship with him, with the other apostles, and with the Father and the Son. Fellowship involves simply a joint participation, a sharing. But John knew that a Christian could walk in sin, for he wrote, "If we say that we have fellowship with Him, and walk in darkness, we lie, and do not the truth" (v. 6). How could the apostle ever forget the boast of Simon Peter to Christ, "If I should die with Thee, I will not deny Thee in any way" (Mark 14:31). But John himself was included in the error, for the Spirit of God was careful to include these words in the inspired record, "Likewise also said they all" (Mark 14:31).

Which of us has not made a similar boast on some occasion, either audibly or deep within the recesses of the heart? But then came the test, the pressure! How soon, impelled by the old nature and allured by the world, we left the realm of light and stepped into darkness! Please do not misunderstand. I am not suggesting that a true believer could ever lose his salvation. But when we sin, our fellowship with God is broken. The child of light then becomes a "Christian out of character."

If we should ever claim to have fellowship with Christ while living disobediently and willfully, two things about us are true. First, according to John, "we lie." We may not intend to be untruthful, but walking in darkness is in itself a practical lie. Alexander Maclaren said, "It is a pity that a man should hold his head so high that he does not look to keep his feet out of the mud." If we profess fellowship with God while walking in darkness, we are acting out an untruth. Our lives are a practical falsehood.

Second, the truth of God is not really being practiced in our lives. John said, "We lie, and do not the truth." As a result, fellowship is broken with the One who is the light.

Inconsistency in the Christian life probably does more damage to the faith and testimony of the church than any other failure. A young lady who works in a professional office told me she was delighted to learn in her first week on the job that one of her fellow workers was also a Christian. She expected that together they would be an effective witness for Christ. But she was soon dismayed. Even though that other employee often boasted of her faith, her words and deeds indicated that she had deviated from the light and was walking in darkness. Ill-tempered remarks, misrepresentations of the facts, poor treatment of fellow workers—all these and more indicated that her profession of fellowship with God was a falsehood. "If we say that we have fellowship with Him, and walk in darkness, we lie, and do not the truth" (v. 6).

FELLOWSHIP AND CLEANSING (v. 7)
The Spirit of God teaches clearly the one condition for continuing fellowship with the Heavenly Father: ". . . if we walk in the light, as He is in the light . . ." (v. 7) . Remember, the

status of our salvation is not in view here, but our fellowship with the Father and His Son. If we are to maintain the best relationship with Him, we must walk in holiness.

"But," you ask, "just what is this walk in the light?" Good question! If it is the one essential to unhindered fellowship, every believer should want to know exactly what it involves. And he should strive to practice it in every facet of his experience.

To walk in the light is to live in complete openness toward God. The psalmist said, "He who dwelleth in the secret place of the Most High shall abide under the shadow of the Almighty" (Psalm 91:1). Every Israelite knew that "the secret place of the Most High" was the holy of holies in the tabernacle and temple—the place where God manifested His presence. That's where Aaron the high priest represented Israel before Jehovah. God dwelt there in the midst of His people. The shekinah, the light of glory, flashed from between the cherubim, which were located over the blood-sprinkled mercy seat.

In the virtue of that applied blood, Aaron could stand "in the light." A great veil hung between the holy place and the holy of holies, keeping all except him from entering. Even so, every godly Israelite knew with absolute certainty that God was abiding there with His people. Therefore, every area of his life—labor and rest, waking and sleeping, thought and action—was tested by the presence of God.

The high priest had fellowship with God *in the light* by entering into His presence in the holy of holies. Today every believer in Christ has that same privilege of fellowship! The veil has been rent from top to bottom. The glory of God is now seen in the person of the Lord Jesus. We are to walk in the light; that is, we are to expose every facet of our lives to Christ. His truth reveals and illumines. Walking in the light, therefore, means opening ourselves unreservedly to God and His Word—just as Aaron walked into the light of shekinah.

Notice, please, that this verse does *not* say, "If we walk *according to* the light." It lays down no conditions. If it did, no Christian would be in fellowship with God—for none of us can live a perfect, sinless life. The question is not *how* we walk but *where* we walk. And where is that? "In the light." When our hearts are open to the Light, we are willing to judge as wrong anything that is not in keeping with that light. If some action, word, or thought is not right, we will expose and confess it, then put it away.

John wrote in his second epistle, "I rejoiced greatly that I found of thy children walking in truth" (2 John 4). In his third letter he exclaimed, "I have no greater joy than to hear that my children walk in truth" (3 John 4). This, I believe, is the same as walking in the light. God's truth shines upon us, and we do not draw back from it. We let it expose our sins and wrong motives. We do not hide from God; we do not walk in the dark. Just as Aaron in the most holy place was revealed for exactly what he was, so the believer, enjoying fellowship as he walks in the light, does not draw back from the revealing truth of God's Word upon his heart. Not one of us stands sinless. But when we are walking in the light, we are willing for the sin to be made known and ready to renounce it.

MEASURING UP

John said that we are to "walk in the light as *He* is in the light." But how can we possibly measure up to the pattern of Christ? Consider Aaron as he stands before the Lord in the most holy place. All the time he is there in the light, the blood upon that mercy seat is, in type, cleansing him from all sin. Just so, the New Testament believer has the constant and continuing efficacy of Christ's atoning work. The light reveals our sin, and the blood of the Lord Jesus continually cleanses it.

An important fact must be noted here: The same verb tense used in verse 3 for "have fellowship" appears in the phrase "cleanseth us" (v. 7). If the child of God is to have abiding fellowship with God and cleansing by Him, he must meet the condition of walking in the light. All the while we are within that circle of light, "the blood of Jesus Christ . . . cleanseth us from all sin." Not only does the blood shed in propitiation for our sins open the way into the presence of God, but also there in the light of that presence it continues to cleanse from the sin that it reveals. A. C. Gaebelein stated it well: "Walking in the light shows us what we are, and we cannot say that we have no sin. But we have no consciousness of sin *resting* upon us before a holy God. Though we know that sin is in us, we have the assurance of being cleansed from it by Christ's precious blood. Such is the blessed position of a true Christian."

Christ's sacrifice is God's basis for fellowship. By faith we have been taken into His communion. As sinners cleansed, we have new life. We stand in the full value of the blood of Jesus Christ. So fellowship, a mutual sharing with Him, is ours as we allow our lives to be searched, exposed by the light of His truth and presence. We walk there. As we do, sweet fellowship with the Father is enjoyed, and the Savior's sacrifice, with all of its efficacy, keeps us cleansed and pure.

> Walk in the light, so shalt thou know
>   That fellowship of love
> His Spirit only can bestow
>   Who reigns in light above.
> Walk in the light, o'er sin abhorred
>   Thou shalt the victory gain;
> The blood of Jesus Christ thy Lord
>   Cleanseth from every stain.
> Walk in the light, and thou shalt find
>   Thy heart made truly His
> Who dwells in cloudless light enshrined
>   In whom no darkness is.

Where are *you* walking, child of God? Is your life transparent, open to the light? Are you responding with childlike spirit to the Father's correction? Or are you complacent? Very lenient with yourself? Fellowship with the Father and the Son can continue only as you walk in the light. Open your life to God. Then you'll know again the truth of the poem that began this chapter. "Fellowship divine, O what blessed sweet communion!"

1 John 1:8-10

If we say that we have no sin, we deceive ourselves, and the truth is not in us.

If we confess our sins, He is faithful and just to forgive us our sins, and to cleanse us from all unrighteousness.

If we say that we have not sinned, we make Him a liar, and His word is not in us.

3

Broken Fellowship

A friend of mine often says, "Treating sin lightly is like stroking the head of a tiger and saying 'nice kitty.'" Yet our day is marked by many Christians who are doing exactly that! Current permissive trends have tended to brainwash many of God's people into an insensitivity to sin. As a result, some believers are habitually and willfully breaking God's moral laws and suffering spiritual harm. True, nothing can deprive the believer of eternal life—but even the smallest sin can distract or hinder his fellowship with Christ.

In the opening verses of this epistle, John stated firmly that there can be no communion with God apart from the light. Fellowship with the Father is the essential characteristic of the new life we receive when we are born again. His will is that we walk in the light as His dear children.

Every believer therefore must keep his heart

open to the searching beams of God's Word. As he does, the Holy Spirit will reveal every deed, every motive, every thought that is outside the realm of light. To shut out the convicting work of the Spirit is to invite God's strong disfavor. We dare not be nonchalant about sin!

Every believer should be walking in the light. Yet the apostle indicated that a Christian can be deceived into falling back to the darkness. This might occur in several ways. In the preceding verses, John pointed out one form of deception: that to claim fellowship with God while letting iniquity abide in the heart and life is to lie (v. 6). We may fool those around us, and may even be successful in deluding ourselves, but God knows the heart. He cannot be deceived.

THE PERIL OF SELF-DECEPTION (v. 8)
The apostle now brings to our attention another kind of deception: "If we say that we have no sin, we deceive ourselves, and the truth is not in us" (1 John 1:8). The believer walking in the light will honestly admit that the potential for committing sin is still a part of his person and character. Knox translated this verse as follows: "Sin is with us; if we deny that, we are cheating ourselves; it means that truth is not in us." To claim the absence of sin in our lives, therefore, is to violate the truth of God's Word.

When the apostle says "sin" here, to what is he referring? Is he accusing the one who claims to be without sin of deliberate hypocrisy? I think not. Remember, he has just declared that "the blood of Jesus Christ, His Son, cleanseth us from all sin" (v. 7). To say "I have no sin" would be a denial of this provision of God's salvation.

I believe that the "sin" the apostle is talking about is the old sin nature. Even though we are saved, it still dwells actively within and motivates our actual misdeeds. It is incorrect to say, "Since the blood of Christ has cleansed me from all sin, I no longer have this condition within." But let's face it. Even though we are saved, the flesh is just as far from perfection as it was before we received the Savior. The old nature is still very much with us!

The apostle Paul testified to this in his epistle to the Romans when he confessed, "For I know that in me (that is, in my flesh) dwelleth no good thing; for to will is present with me, but how to perform that which is good I find not" (Romans 7:18). Regeneration is *not* the improving of the flesh, the old sinful nature; but rather, it is the implantation of new life from above.

No doubt the claim of having no sin stems from spiritual pride. We tend to revel in the satisfaction of our new standing before God. We "shine the halo," trying to put on a front that will give credence to the assertion that there is no sin in us. The claim is absurd. It's comparable to Peter's response when he was commanded of the Lord to take and eat what he saw in his vision. He said, "Not so, Lord" (Acts 10:14). We have already seen that claiming Christ as Master and Lord while refusing to obey Him is an incongruity. Just so, the claim of any Christian that he has no sin is equally an impossibility.

In fact, if we maintain that we are free from all sin, John says "we deceive ourselves, and the truth is not in us" (v. 8). God calls for "truth in the inward parts" (Psalm 51:6). The one who describes himself as being without sin is running the risk of walking in darkness and thereby being removed from fellowship with God who is light. How much we need this warning of Paul: "For if a man think himself to be something, when he is nothing, he deceiveth himself" (Galatians 6:3).

There is a further danger. The Christian who is ignorant of the old nature, and is blind to its power to assert itself, will soon be victimized by his own self-delusion. He is headed for a fall! The truth of God must always be allowed to operate within us so that we are not deceived. We have only to look at the godly characters of both the Old and New Testaments to see that they too had the opposing forces of light and darkness locked in conflict within. It's exactly as Paul said,

> For the flesh lusteth against the Spirit, and
> the Spirit against the flesh; and these are con-
> trary the one to the other, so that ye cannot
> do the things that ye would (Galatians 5:17).

A WRONG ASSUMPTION

Sometimes a believer who sins will simply dismiss the matter from his conscience by saying, "The blood of Christ cleanses me from all sin, so I don't have to worry about it." This assumption is in error! It overlooks the important sequence of spiritual truths given in verse 9, "If we confess our sins, He is faithful and just to forgive us our sins, and to cleanse us from all unrighteousness" (1 John 1:9).

To harmonize the truth of the cleansing blood (v. 7) with the call for confession followed by forgiveness and cleansing (v. 9), you must turn your attention to an illustration from the Old Testament. On the day of atonement, the sin-offering was presented before Jehovah by the high priest on behalf of Israel. We're told,

> For on that day shall the priest make an atonement for you, to cleanse you, that ye may be clean from all your sins before the Lord (Leviticus 16:30).

The Israelite was able to live before Jehovah another year because of the cleansing blood of this sin-offering. As Christians, we also stand unashamed before God because of a great sin-offering—the death of the Lord Jesus. We can ever claim, "The blood of Jesus Christ, His Son, cleanseth us from all sin."

But another question arises. What about those daily transgressions, those acts of sin an Israelite committed after the day of atonement? Was any provision made for these? Yes. A ritual of purification was provided for those who became contaminated or unclean (see Numbers 19:1-10). Because of the cleansing blood of the day of atonement, the Israelite could stand before God as He dwelt in the shekinah in the midst of His people. But he could also be cleansed from daily defilement through the purification rite of the ashes of the red heifer. Likewise, the New Testament believer is accepted before God because of the continuing efficacy of the blood of the Lamb. Provision is made for any transgression, any sin against God, by His child as he travels the pilgrim pathway. In 1 John 1:9, John tells us what that provision is.

A READY CONFESSION (v. 9)

A Christian cannot claim that he has no sin. He therefore must recognize that even though iniquity does exist in his life as a fact, it need not interfere with his fellowship with God. The divine standard is this: "He that saith he abideth in Him ought himself also so to walk, even as He walked" (1 John 2:6). Who would dare to measure himself by *that* standard! Who would not admit that he falls far short of it! Yes, every believer is guilty of sinning, and verse 9 outlines the procedure for cleansing.

Keep in mind, however, that 1 John 1:9 is written exclusively to all believers. I have sometimes heard sincere Christians quote this verse to unconverted people, urging them to "confess their sins." But this inspired epistle was addressed only to saints, children in the family of God. The provision of confession and forgiveness is exclusively for them.

Let us suppose for a moment that a letter has been sent to a specific church in a certain city. Would any in the town who did *not* belong to that church imagine that the instructions, admonitions, and exhortations were intended for them? Of course not! When the Christians who received this Spirit-inspired epistle heard the words read in their assembly, "If we confess our sins, He is faithful and just to forgive us our sins, and to cleanse us from all unrighteousness," they knew immediately that John meant believers. This provision of confession and forgiveness was *never* intended for the unbeliever. If all he needed to do to be assured of forgiveness and cleansing were to confess his sins, quite obviously he would not have to be told of Christ's death on the cross. He wouldn't have to hear of his need for faith in the crucified and risen Redeemer. But it's *not* that way. My friend, this is *God's family primer*. It's addressed to the "little born ones," those who are already saved.

THE PROVISIONS EXPLAINED

What then is the provision for the sinning child of God? The apostle John tells believers who have fallen into iniquity that they can be restored to the light of God's favor. They are to come to Him "as dear children," confessing their sins.

"Confess." What an important word! It comes from two Greek terms joined together. One of them means "to speak" and the other means "the same." To "confess" therefore means "to speak the same as, to agree with." To confess our sins is not simply agreeing with what some other Christian says about them. He may excuse them! Or he may compare our transgressions with his own. Rather, we must agree *with God* about our sins. And this cannot be done unless we allow God's Word to penetrate our hearts and reveal our sins for exactly what they are. When we "speak the same thing" about a sin to

God as He does to us, we are truly confessing. If sin is committed, confession must follow. Kenneth Sheppard said this is "not necessarily a ritualistic listing or recitation of sins committed, but an honest agreement of heart with God about that which stopped the flow of fellowship between the two. It is openness with God about the issues, not trying to hide anything from God by not owning up to it. It is to confess that we failed to walk in the light."

Christian friend, this is vastly deeper and more real than simply asking for forgiveness in a general way. In fact, we are not even told in this verse to ask God to forgive us, because this would imply that God needed to be asked. Instead, we are to judge ourselves, to determine for ourselves that the thing we have done was in disobedience. The confession of sins in the believer is directed toward God. Fellowship with Him is impossible if we go on accumulating sins and do not confess them. God would be hating the very sins we were allowing, and thus our communion with Him would be broken.

A SURE RESPONSE

Broken fellowship *can* be restored to the sinning saint. As the believer becomes aware of his sin through his conscience, he must agree with God concerning it. This is a family matter! Remember, it does not involve our standing before God as redeemed ones, because we have been "accepted in the Beloved" (Ephesians 1:6). But it hinders our fellowship.

I vividly recall more than one occasion when I

disobeyed my father and tried to camouflage the transgression. It always brought upon me the chastening rod—and in our home it was the razor strop! My father did not disown me; nor did I cease to be his son. But he did punish me. Memories also crowd my heart of times when I acted contrary to my father's desires, but I acknowledged and confessed them without his prodding. How welcome the absence of punishment and the assurance of forgiveness!

In the family of God, fellowship is broken by sin. God will not fellowship with us until confession is made. Then God acts faithfully and righteously to restore that broken fellowship.

God stands by His Word. Note please that John did not say in this context that God is *"loving* and gracious to forgive us." He is that; but here His *faithfulness* and *justice* are indicated. When a child of God acknowledges his sin to the Father, he can be assured that because God in His very nature is just and faithful, He will forgive that sin.

Is God unrighteous for offering forgiveness so freely? Don't think that for a moment! He *must* punish sin. But His righteousness is maintained in forgiveness because the punishment for that sin has already been borne by His Son. The penalty of the believer's sins was met at Calvary. God the Father can righteously forgive His children's sins because the work of His Son at Calvary is sufficient to atone for them.

Not only does God "forgive us our sins" when we agree with Him concerning them, He also "cleanses us from all unrighteousness." Suppose, friend, some sin is lurking within your heart, forgotten or unknown. Certainly you cannot confess that which you do not know. How gracious the provision of our Heavenly Father! He is not only faithful and just to forgive us the sins we confess, but also to "cleanse us from *all* unrighteousness."

These words of our Lord Jesus to Peter are significant: "If I wash thee not, thou hast no part with Me" (John 13:8). That "part" we have with Christ is fellowship, and it's only possible when there is forgiveness and cleansing. God not only forgives, He also takes away the defilement. Paul said, "That He might sanctify and cleanse it with the washing of water by the word" (Ephesians 5:26).

What an appeal for keeping nothing back from God! Instead of being afraid of Him or shying away from Him, we can have happy, open fellowship with Him. This demands from us an openness to the light of His Word, a ready confession of sins, and a cleansing from all sin through the blood of Christ.

Before concluding this chapter, let me issue a word of caution: Once you have confessed your sins to the Lord, leave them there. You do not have to go back repeatedly to confess that same transgression. Of course, if the sin is committed again, it must again be confessed. But once you do, you're forgiven and cleansed. Donald Grey Barnhouse suggested, "To go back . . . again and again is to act like a dog who digs a bone which he has buried. The Savior never nags His children; it is Satan who nags the conscience. The God of all grace fully cleanses His child. Do not, then, play dog and dig up what was buried by our Lord."

If you are guilty of hiding some sin from God, rationalizing some misdeed, or simply excusing yourself on the basis of "weakness," take direct action right now. Agree with God concerning your sin. Come to Him in the openness of confession. Claim His promise of forgiveness and cleansing. Then that blessed fellowship with Him that was disturbed by sin will be restored!

1 John 2:1,2

My little children, these things write I unto you, that ye sin not. And if any man sin, we have an advocate with the Father, Jesus Christ the righteous;

And He is the propitiation for our sins, and not for ours only, but also for the sins of the whole world.

4
The Disobedient Child Restored

Suppose a teenager who has grown up in a closely knit family, and who understands its regulations well, suddenly begins to break the rules. She sasses her mother, deliberately stays out past curfew, and refuses to do her expected part of the household chores. What happens? The unity and harmony of the family is disrupted. Relationships are strained and communication breaks down. The wayward one senses her father's disfavor. Pressure mounts. The precious intimacy, support, and love which has existed within that family circle is strained. Fellowship is broken.

So it is in the family of God. The grand theme that runs through the entire first epistle of John is *fellowship*—fellowship with God in and through Christ. Only children in the family, those who are born again, can enjoy this happy privilege. The overall design the apostle established at the beginning of the epistle is this:

". . . that ye also may have fellowship with us;
and truly our fellowship is with the Father, and
with His Son, Jesus Christ." It is impossible for
the unsaved to enjoy this fellowship, for they
are dead in trespasses and sins.

As the believer begins his new life with
Christ, he is soon faced with the question: What
happens when I sin and my fellowship with
God is broken? The answer is given in 1 John
1:9, as we saw in the preceding chapter. Then
follows a more important question: How can a
holy God restore a sinning child?

When the child of God finds that communion
with the Lord is broken temporarily by disobedience, he learns that the Father has already
established a solid basis for restoration. First,
full provision has been made for the erring child
in the all-sufficient, cleansing blood of the
Savior. "The blood of Jesus Christ . . . cleanseth
us from *all* sin" (1 John 1:7). Because God's
justice is satisfied in the Savior's death on the
cross, and because He is faithful to His Word,
He forgives and cleanses the confessing child.

A second basis upon which the children of
the Heavenly Father are restored to fellowship
is found in 1 John 2:1,2.

My little children, these things write I unto
you, that ye sin not. And if any man sin,
we have an advocate with the Father, Jesus
Christ the righteous (1 John 2:1).

The Lord Jesus makes possible our restored
fellowship by His intercession on our behalf. He
does this on the merit of His work on Calvary.
Someone might object that this gracious provi-

sion would cause the child of God to be lax toward sin and to tolerate it in his own life. But the apostle answered this objection by the emphatic manner in which he stated the terms for forgiveness, cleansing, and restoration.

The passage before us is one of the most precious and crucial of the entire New Testament. May the Spirit of God illumine and touch your heart as we consider it together.

GOD'S STANDARD (v. 1)

Educators and parents have learned the value of setting high but realistic expectation levels for children. The Lord's standard for His family is established in these words: "My little children, these things write I unto you, *that ye sin not*" (1 John 2:1). The apostle Paul stated in Romans 3, that God is just in declaring the believing sinner righteous. Then in chapter 6 the rhetorical question is put forth, "Shall we sin, then?" His answer, "God forbid!" In these verses in 1 John there can be found *no reason* in God's work of forgiveness that would ever give license to sin. C. H. Spurgeon said, "Those men who think that God's grace, when fully, fairly, and plainly preached, will lead men into sin, know not what they say nor whereof they affirm. It is neither according to nature nor to grace for men to find an argument for sin in the goodness of God."

God has but one standard for His children: "that ye sin not." The purpose of the apostle in setting forth the glorious truths of this passage, truths to be received experientially in the life of the believer, is just the opposite from what some have supposed. In fact, it is one of the strongest scriptural statements *against sin* in the entire Bible!

C. I. Scofield once preached a sermon entitled "The Abounding Grace of God." When he was finished, a man approached him and said, "If I believed as you do, I would go out and have my fill of sin." Scofield looked squarely into the face of this uninstructed, misguided Christian and replied, "Child of God, just how much sin would it take to fill you?" The man's emphasis was totally wrong. He was looking for license to sin.

The apostle's primary purpose for writing on this subject was that the "little children" should proceed in the Christian life with every anticipation of success—not of failure. If we walk in open, transparent fellowship with God, we will not sin. Regrettably, many Christians expect to fall into transgression. But let me say it clearly, unmistakably, *dogmatically*—there is no excuse, no allowance, no need, no right, no license to sin!

Kenneth Wuest's expanded translation of Romans 6:1 is this: "What shall we say then? Shall we habitually abide under the control of sin in order that this grace previously mentioned may be increasingly lavished on us? Far be the thought! Such as we, who died once for all with reference to sin, how is it possible for us to exist in the grip of its motivating energy any longer?" The entreaty to the believer (sometimes a command) to "sin not" is therefore not John's alone. The apostle Paul said, "Awake to righteousness, and *sin not*; for some have not the knowledge of God" (1 Corinthians 15:34). This is also the thrust of Peter's command, "But, as He who hath called you is holy, so be ye holy in all manner of life, because it is written, Be ye holy; for I am holy" (1 Peter 1:15,16). As children in the family of God, bearing the likeness of the Father and indwelt by His Spirit, we can adopt no lesser standard. Our aim must be to remove all sin from our lives.

This high goal, set by God and written by the apostle John, is presented as a loving plea, not a slavish dictum. John was the last living member of the 12 disciples. He was speaking with affection to his beloved readers. Very possibly he was thinking of that night in the upper room when our Lord described His future work as our Advocate. He spoke of His disciples in the same affectionate term John used here, *teknia*, "little children." According to W. E. Vine, this was a word used by a loving teacher to his students when the circumstance required a tender appeal. Therefore, a word which our Lord used only once in speaking to His disciples, and that just before He was to leave them, was the very same word the apostle John used to address these believers—and us. The appeal for the Christian to his highest and holiest ambition, that he sin not, came in sensitive terms of affection and compassion, not as a harsh, cold pronouncement.

Child of God, what is your heart's response to this standard? Because you belong to Him, you are righteous in your *position* in Christ. And you are to *practice* holiness. An old saint said, "He that falls into sin is a man; he that grieves

at sin is a saint; he that boasts of sin is a devil."
The sad plight of Christendom today is that sin
is excused by the attitude, "We must learn to
live with it." Christian friend, take the high
road! Robert Candlish said, "The very object of
all that the apostle writes on the subject is that,
at the very least, we rise to the high and holy attitude of determining not to sin."

OUR ADVOCATE

What if John had stopped with the word "that
ye sin not"? Believers would be in a hopeless
predicament. But he went on to tell us that God
has also made provision for us if we do sin.
Mind you, he is not giving an allowance for sin,
but a means of restoration if we do. Note that
the apostle said, "And *if* any man sin" (v. 1).
We might think that he should have said,
"*When* any man sins." But he didn't want to imply that we have to sin.

If the child of God does sin, what is the
remedy? What has God done to restore His sinning child? Surely, as previously noted, we can
confess our sins and be forgiven (1 John 1:9).
But we also need One who can plead our case.
We have, as J. N. Darby gives it in his translation, "a patron with the Father." In ancient
Rome a patron was one who maintained the interest of his clients in every way. He was an in-
fluential man who protected, directed, and
promoted the welfare of certain people. John
says, "We have an advocate with the Father,
Jesus Christ the righteous." Seated at the
Father's right hand in the heavenlies, the Savior
is our patron, always at work on our behalf.

Interestingly, this word "advocate" is the very same word used by Christ of the Holy Spirit when He said, "And I will pray the Father, and He shall give you another *Comforter*" (John 14:16). He promised us another helper. The Greek word is *paracletos*, which means "intercessor" or "helper." The Holy Spirit is now our advocate on earth; Christ is our advocate in Heaven with the Father, where He now appears "in the presence of God for us" (Hebrews 9:24).

Christ not only intercedes for us when we repent and seek restoration, He is also our advocate while we are sinning. This work is part of the continuing ministry of our Great Shepherd, the Lord Jesus. How is it that a believer is not cast away and lost when he sins? What would happen if Christ did not hold us in that same embrace of love with which He first received us? We would have no hope! But at the Father's right hand we have an advocate, the Lord Jesus. And the efficacy of His work in Heaven on our behalf is guaranteed by His righteousness, and by His finished work at Calvary.

When we sin, Satan, called in Scripture the "accuser of the brethren," comes before God and points the finger of blame at us. Praise God, we have One who is our advocate before the Father, and with the Father, even while we sin! A biblical illustration is the case of Simon Peter. The Lord had said to him, "Simon, Simon, behold, Satan hath desired to have you, that he may sift you as wheat; but I have prayed for thee, that thy faith fail not" (Luke 22:31,32).

True, Peter did deny the Lord, but his faith *did not fail*! He was still a child of God, a disciple of the Lord Jesus. How different from Judas! When he betrayed Christ, he "went out and hanged himself." But Jesus looked at Peter, and the erring disciple "went out and wept bitterly."

Not only did Christ pray for Simon Peter, He restored him to fellowship. Following His resurrection, we are told that "He was seen of Cephas, then of the twelve" (1 Corinthians 15:5). And Luke wrote, "The Lord is risen indeed, and hath appeared to Simon" (Luke 24:34). The sin was not held against Peter, and he and the Master were in full communion once again. The Lord Jesus had demonstrated His Work as advocate in the upper room when He took a basin of water and a towel and washed the disciples' feet. He said to Peter, "If I wash thee not, thou hast no part with Me" (John 13:8). Wayward, dirty feet must be placed in His hands, "If any man sin, we have an advocate. . . ." He will restore them to cleanliness by His love.

The believing sinner needs the "washing of regeneration" (Titus 3:5) only once. But whenever fellowship is broken by sin, the obedient Christian is in need of that cleansing which Christ alone can accomplish through His advocacy with the Father. Despite his sin, Peter was restored. The results are evidenced later in his life when he did indeed "strengthen his brethren" by becoming the mighty spokesman on the day of Pentecost. He proceeded to do exactly what the risen Lord had commanded when they stood beside the fire of coals on the seashore. Christ had said, "Feed My sheep" (John 21:16). Peter had learned the practical effect of that which Christ had pictured as He washed the disciples' feet. Restored to fellowship, he served God mightily.

No effort of our own, not even our confession of sin, will bring about our cleansing unless we have an advocate. We are not to straighten out our lives first in order to come to Him. We are to come to Him as we are, dirty feet and all, to be washed and restored. Christ Himself is the One who cleanses. He abides in Heaven right now as the righteous One, our representative before God—just as He was our Substitute and Surety on the cross. Sin interrupts communion; our Advocate restores it. Thomas Brooks told of a Christian woman who in great conflict said to Satan, "Reason not with me, I am but a weak woman; if thou hast anything to say, say it to my Christ. He is my Advocate, my strength, and my Redeemer; and He shall plead for me."

How comforting for the believer to learn that Christ is his advocate with the Father! This gives us the immediate and full assurance that we do not cease to be the children of God when we sin. By this we know we are still His sons and daughters, and He is still our Father. We may become defiled, but the Christ who saved and brought us into the Father's house will see to the washing of our feet. He will love us unto the end, for our fellowship is "with the Father, and with His Son, Jesus Christ" (1 John 1:3).

OUR PROPITIATION (v. 2)
But you may ask, "On what basis does God

restore His sinning child? It is true that our Advocate sits at the Father's right hand, ever living to make intercession for us! But how are our sins to be cleansed? On what basis are they forgiven?" 1 John 2:2 tells us. "And He is the propitiation for our sins, and not for ours only, but also for the sins of the whole world."

Just what is "propitiation"? Here is Scofield's definition: "Propitiation is that Godward aspect of Christ's death which satisfies the whole demand of the law upon the sinner, opens the way for God righteously to meet in Christ, God's mercy seat, every sinner who believes." Through Christ's work at Calvary, God's wrath is turned away. He can then look upon us with favor and receive us without violating His holiness.

The Father's love flows unhindered to us because of the atoning death of His Son. Speaking of Christ, the apostle wrote, "Whom God hath set forth to be a propitiation through faith in His blood, to declare His righteousness for the remission of sins that are past, through the forbearance of God" (Romans 3:25). Here in 1 John 2:2 and again in 1 John 4:10, Christ is said to be "the propitiation for our sins." A similar Greek word is used in Hebrews 9:5 and is translated "mercy seat." Therefore, the Old Testament picture of God having His wrath satisfied, of being merciful to the sinner, is pictured by the blood-sprinkled mercy seat. It was "the place of covering." The priest took the blood of the bullock and sprinkled it upon the mercy seat and before the ark of the covenant. It was then possible for God to meet with Israel, because the blood had covered their sins.

Christ has become the meeting place of a holy God and the believing sinner. The Lord Jesus is not only the Lamb for sinners slain, He is also the altar of atonement and the blood-sprinkled mercy seat. When He appears as our advocate with the Father, He is also the propitiation for our sins. Christ and His death are the ground whereby God is made favorably disposed toward us. This is illustrated in 2 Samuel 9:7, which tells us the basis for David's kind treatment of Mephibosheth.

As David was kind toward Mephibosheth because of his love for his father Jonathan, so God looks with favor upon us because of our identification with Christ. In the virtue of His propitiation at Calvary, His expiatory death on our behalf, God's wrath is turned away. He is therefore able to forgive the sin and restore His erring child. When we sin, we are forgiven *for Christ's sake.* The sin is not being overlooked by God; its punishment was paid in the death of His Son. Christ atoned for that sin by the shedding of His blood.

No Christian may sin cheaply. Knowing that we have an advocate to rely on, and understanding that God is faithful and just to forgive sin and cleanse all unrighteousness, gives us no cause to play "fast and loose" with sin. The very fact of Christ's sacrifice should in itself engender in the heart of the believer a holy hatred for sin and a consuming desire to please the Father. John said, "My little children, these things write I unto you, that ye sin not."

1 John 2:3-11

And by this we do know that we know Him, if we keep His commandments.

He that saith, I know Him, and keepeth not His commandments, is a liar, and the truth is not in him.

But whosoever keepeth His word, in him verily is the love of God perfected; by this know we that we are in Him.

He that saith he abideth in Him ought himself also so to walk, even as He walked.

Brethren, I write no new commandment unto you, but an old commandment which ye had from the beginning. The old commandment is the word which ye have heard from the beginning.

Again, a new commandment I write unto you, which thing is true in Him and in you, because the darkness is past, and the true light now shineth.

He that saith he is in the light, and hateth his brother, is in darkness even until now.

He that loveth his brother abideth in the light, and there is no occasion of stumbling in him.

But he that hateth his brother is in darkness, and walketh in darkness, and knoweth not where he goeth, because darkness hath blinded his eyes.

5
Family Examination Time

If God is light and love—and He is—it naturally follows that everyone born of God by the Holy Spirit will express those same qualitys of righteousness and love. One of the threads of truth running Epistle of 1 John is, "Christ our life." And if indeed this "eternal life, which was with the Father, and manifested into us" (1 John 1:2), does dwell within, then the characteristics of our Heavenly Father will also be seen in us.

Although by comparison the new life shows through us rather feebly at times, it will be manifested just the same. Consistently in this letter, therefore, the apostle reminds us that God puts the profession that we are His children to the test. If we are truly in the light, the consequences will be seen in the way we live.

My friend, it's examination time! In the passage before us, the apostle John suggested three tests for evaluating our profession. Each is introduced by the words, "He that saith . . ." (vv. 4,6,9). (1) If we are in the light, we will keep

God's commandments. (2) If we are in the light, the blood avails for us. (3) If we are in the light, we have the confidence that stems from a practical walk with God.

The apostle Peter said, "Wherefore the rather, brethren, give diligence to make your calling and election sure" (2 Peter 1:10). As believers, we have the assurance that God "knoweth them that are His" (2 Timothy 2:19). But we in turn must walk so that the witness of the Spirit will be clear and positive within us. Fellowship results from walking in light. If we are in the light, the consequences will be evident in us. As you think about these three tests with me, ask the Holy Spirit to examine your own heart. Then, make the necessary adjustments.

THE TEST OF OBEDIENCE (vv. 3-5)
Do you recall the idle boast of school days when you declared, "I'll tell you one thing, I *know* my history lesson"? Then came the exam. Absolute knowledge was required. It had been a simple matter to profess the confidence, but now the examination would prove the reality. John wrote, "And by this we do know that we know Him, if we *keep* His commandments" (v. 3).

The apostle John was speaking of far more than mere intellectual assent. He used the word "know" in much the same way the apostle Paul used it in his epistles. It transcends intellectual comprehension, which very likely would be possible for an unregenerate man. But none can have an understanding of God, none can have a personal experience with Him unless there is life. Paul wrote, "For God, who commanded the light to shine out of darkness, hath shone in our hearts, to give the light of the knowledge of the glory of God in the face of Jesus Christ" (2 Corinthians 4:6). John's use of the perfect tense of the verb "to know" causes the verse to have this meaning: "And by this we do know that *we have come to know Him and continue to know Him. . . ."* This knowledge includes personal experience and spiritual certainty. And what is the experience? Our daily walk: the way we live.

Life always expresses itself. In a physical sense, you don't have to say, "Today I am going to try to act like I'm alive." If the body possesses physical life, that life will be evidenced by speech, action, and movement.

Spiritual life also expresses itself. Without the new life, we could not understand God nor could we know Him. The Lord Jesus, after claiming that God was His Father, said, "The Son can do nothing of Himself, but what He seeth the Father do; for whatever things He doeth, these also doeth the Son in the same manner" (John 5:19). Christ had the mind of the Father, and He acted and spoke accordingly. He could do nothing of Himself—nothing apart from the Father. This is the best proof that Christ and the Father are one.

If we keep God's Word, His commandments, we are of the same life with Him. Following His example springs from having the same nature, the same life. We show that we know God by keeping His Word. Each involves the other; we cannot know without doing. The author of Hebrews wrote,

Though He were a Son, yet learned He obedience by the things which He suffered;

And being made perfect, He became the author of eternal salvation unto all them that obey Him (Hebrews 5:8,9).

The practical obedience of a genuine believer is contrasted with the statement of the man who claims to know Christ, yet "keepeth not His commandments . . ." (1 John 2:4). To claim the knowledge of God yet disobey Him is an unresolvable contradiction. The evidence and the assurance that one knows God is simple obedience to His Word. James asked a sticky question when he wrote, "What doth it profit, my brethren, though a man say he hath faith, and have not works?" (James 2:14). Paul spoke of just such a person in his letter to Titus, "They profess that they know God, but in works they deny Him" (Titus 1:16). If we are not keeping His commandments, our profession of Him must be false. John said that such a person "is a liar, and the truth is not in him" (v. 4).

Much is said today about each having his own "lifestyle." A Christian has but one lifestyle: obedience to God's Word. Any profession of faith that fails to be corroborated by a Christlike walk immediately marks that one as living a lie.

The practical testing of our faith not only determines the reality of our relationship with God but also of our position. Note that the scope of "keeping" God's Word involves more than just the commandments (v. 5). The "whole counsel of God" is revealed in His Word. When we are true to it, doing our best to obey it, we experience this twofold blessing:

1. God's love is fulfilled in us. "In him verily is the love of God perfected." James spoke of a faith perfected by works; here John's emphasis is on a *love perfected by obedience*. The same truth is found in John's gospel: "He that hath My commandments, and keepeth them, he it is that loveth Me; and he that loveth Me shall be loved of My Father, and I will love him, and will manifest Myself to him" (John 14:21). When the Word of God is obeyed, the mind of Christ is formed in us.

2. We have assurance of our standing. "By this know we that we are in Him" (v. 5). As we follow Christ, the security of our position in Him is verified. Not only do we have the knowledge of the Lord Jesus; we are also *in Him*. Cheerful obedience to God's Word is the proof that our knowledge of Him is valid and our position in His family is genuine.

The word of the risen Christ to the church of Philadelphia, communicated by the apostle John himself, strongly emphasized this critical point. And the Lord Jesus had stressed the same truth in the last discourse to His disciples prior to His death. What was it? "Thou hast kept My Word." This is the evidence that we know Him, and that we are in Him.

THE TEST OF WALK (v. 6)
The second test in the family examination time is prefaced by the same words as the first, "He that saith. . . ." This is the test of abiding in

Christ. Do you note the progression here? The first was our saving knowledge of Christ and our position in Him; the second is the continuation or the persistence of that knowledge and relationship. A branch abides in the vine so that it can receive the lifegiving sap and as a result flower and bear fruit. The believer too abides in Christ that he may grow strong and become productive.

In order to bring forth fruit, there must be a likeness of nature between the branch and the vine. The Lord Jesus said, "Abide in Me, and I in you. As the branch cannot bear fruit of itself, except it abide in the vine, no more can ye, except ye abide in Me" (John 15:4). John gave the means of determining whether or not one is abiding in God when he indicated that a believer "ought himself also so to walk, even as He [Christ] walked" (v. 6). Phillips paraphrased this verse, "The life of a man who professes to be living in God must bear the stamp of Christ."

What characterized the walk of the Lord Jesus? What makes our walk like His? Now Christian, let me make it clear immediately that I am speaking of *quality, not quantity*. We may be sure that there was infinite capacity in His sinless being for the practice of holiness. Every attribute of the character of God was seen in Jesus Christ, for He was "God manifest in the flesh." And if the very life of Christ dwells in us, and if we abide in Him, that life will manifest itself in the same kind of walk. Remember, John was speaking to "little children," those born into the family of God. No one can begin to follow Christ until he has first received Him as

Savior. How did Christ walk? What qualities of His life will be present in the one abiding in Him? Let me suggest several characteristics of our Savior's walk that should also be true of every member of God's family.

1. *He walked in submission to God's will.* David's words in Psalm 40 are also the testimony of our Lord, "I delight to do Thy will, O my God; yea, Thy law is within my heart" (Psalm 40:8). In the crucible of His suffering, Jesus cried to the Father, "Not My will, but Thine" (Luke 22:42). He was the servant of Jehovah. To be sure, He was the Son, equal but distinct from the Father. As the servant, however, He was subject to the Father. He said, "The Son can do nothing of Himself" and later, "I can of Mine own self do nothing" (John 5:19,30). He voluntarily laid aside His glory and power, and in His sinlessly perfect humanity He was dependent upon His submission to the Father. The command of Scripture is, "Let this mind be in you, which was also in Christ Jesus" (Philippians 2:5).

2. *He walked in obedience to God.* Jesus could say, "The Father hath not left Me alone; for *I do always those things that please Him*" (John 8:29). Again He declared, "I must work the works of Him that sent Me" (John 9:4). The very One who spoke the worlds into being, who commanded, "Let there be light" and there was, walked in humble obedience to the Father.

3. *He walked in humility.* Do you remember these words of our Lord: "I am meek and lowly in heart" (Matthew 11:29)? Both words, "meek" and "lowly," indicate humility. Meekness is

humility toward God; lowliness is humility toward man. Our Lord's submissive attitude toward His fellowman is seen in His relationship with His followers as well as those who were not of the faith. He was slandered and called "a glutton and a winebibber." His enemies questioned His motives. But when He was mocked, "He reviled not again." He willingly humbled Himself that redemption's plan could be fulfilled. Paul wrote of Him:

> Who, being in the form of God, thought it not robbery to be equal with God,
> But made Himself of no reputation, and took upon Him the form of a servant, and was made in the likeness of men;
> And, being found in fashion as a man, He humbled Himself and became obedient unto death, even the death of the cross (Philippians 2:6-8).

Christ's humility was also seen in His relationship to His disciples. John 13 beautifully describes the outworking of this trait in His character. Our Lord said,

> If I, then, your Lord and Master, have washed your feet, ye also ought to wash one another's feet.
> For I have given you an example, that ye should do as I have done to you.
> Verily, verily, I say unto you, The servant is not greater than his lord; neither he that is sent greater than he that sent him.
> If ye know these things, happy are ye if ye do them (John 13:14-17).

4. *He walked in love.* The daily manner of

Christ's demeanor was love. One writer has said that He was "the very personification of benevolence; a man approved of God, that went about doing good." Therefore, the apostle Paul exhorted us to be followers of God, and to "walk in love, as Christ also hath loved us" (Ephesians 5:2). This phase of Jesus' life—walking in love—is also the third test of our profession, to be considered in a moment.

Let me call to your mind these words of our Lord, found in His high priestly prayer to the Father: "As Thou hast sent Me into the world, even so have I also sent them into the world" (John 17:18). If we proclaim that we abide in Christ, then we ought to walk as He walked—in obedience, submission, humility, and love.

THE TEST OF LOVE (vv. 7-11)

The apostle John did not hesitate to use the word "commandment." He was no legalist. He knew that Christ was the fulfillment of the law; the end of the law for righteousness. But he also was fully aware that the dispensation of grace carries with it God's moral law. No true disciple would ever be found neglecting the commandments of our Lord, for they suggest an authority to which every follower of Christ is subject.

John referred to it as an "old commandment" (v. 7). The disciples had possessed it from the beginning; that is, from the time Christ's teaching ministry began. It was part of our Lord's earliest admonition to young Christians, for He had said, "This is My commandment, that ye love one another, as I have loved you"

(John 15:12). He had also told His disciples in the upper room,

> A new commandment I give unto you, that ye love one another; as I have loved you, that ye also love one another.
>
> By this shall all men know that ye are My disciples, if ye have love one to another (John 13:34,35).

Though this commandment is described as "old," it is also new. It is "old" in the sense that Christ's life and word had manifested it. But it is "new" in the sense that this very same life dwells in every believer. It is written *in the heart.* It is new because "the darkness is past, and the true light now shineth" (v. 8).

Because the believer is in the light, he is vitalized with a power that produces in him the same love that was in Christ. A strong spiritual tie of life exists between Christians and Christ; but more than this, it binds one Christian to another. The new life expresses itself in righteousness toward God and love toward man, especially toward one of the *same life.*

This is the test: "He that saith he is in the light, and hateth his brother, is in darkness even until now" (v. 9). How terribly incongruous! The word "brother" is used here to speak of a Christian relationship. There is no universal brotherhood of man and fatherhood of God. We are children of God only through faith in Jesus Christ. If a man says, "I am in the light," he has made a profession. But what is he doing while he is saying that? He's hating his brother! Regardless of any rationalization, any camouflage, the true appraisal of such a man is that he is "in darkness even until now." Up to this moment, notwithstanding any apparent change that took place when he was supposed to have been converted, his unloving walk proves that he is in darkness.

How much insincerity, lack of love, sharp-tongued criticism, and despicable practice would be avoided—would never once show their polluting presence in the assembly of the believers—if we were to face seriously this third test of profession!

The apostle enlarged upon his description of the one who professes to be in the light and yet hates his brother by saying that he "is in darkness, and walketh in darkness, and knoweth not where he goeth, because darkness hath blinded his eyes" (v. 11). When one is truly regenerated and becomes a child of God, practical attitudes should be put away. If they are not, the possession of the new life from above is denied. What sharp lines John draws! Three times the apostle said of the guilty: He is "in darkness," he walks "in darkness," and "darkness hath blinded his eyes" (v. 11).

Commenting on this portion of Scripture, Samuel Ridout said, "It is to be remarked that the apostle, in testing the profession of those who say they know God, does not speak of negative absence of evil, nor of the more general characteristics of what is known as a moral life. He seeks for love, a thing which in its true nature and energy is from God alone. If this be absent, or if in its place there be hatred, it shows the absence of life." In Philippians 3:18, 19, Paul warned of the darkness in which many *professing* Christians are found. If you have professed faith in Christ but your life gives no evidence of the new life and of love, you must seriously ponder these verses and determine whether or not you are still in darkness.

But John concludes with a happy note: "He that loveth his brother abideth in the light, and there is no occasion of stumbling in him" (v. 10). John had already spoken of one who "walks in the light" (1 John 1:7). This verse gives a further progression. The one whose life is characterized by love for his brother "abideth in the light." How blessed the situation of one who loves his brother! This should be the case with every true believer.

If you have an atmosphere of hatred in your heart rather than the true expression of love for your brethren in Christ, you have reason to question the authenticity of what you profess. Indeed, you may not be born again! John said pointedly that not loving one of God's family or what Christ professes is a sign of being in darkness. When we are in the light, we not only see God and are seen of Him, but we see one another and are drawn to each other. Abiding in the light, we do not stumble nor do we put a roadblock in the pathway of others.

This is *like* responding to *like*. As believers, we walk in the light. We keep God's Word. And we love all who have been brought into the light by their faith in Christ. The poet has written,

> Walk in the light! so shalt thou know
> That fellowship of love
> His Spirit only can bestow
> Who reigns in light above.

Walk in the light! and thou shalt own
   Thy darkness passed away,
Because that light hath on thee shone
   In which is perfect day.

                —Bernard Barton

SUMMARY

Christian friends, let's stop for a moment of self-examination. At the beginning of the chapter, we stressed the importance of having our behavior of life be in keeping with what we profess to believe and be. And we review each of three tests of profession John presented, take a moment to evaluate honestly your own conduct and attitude.

First is the test of *obedience.* Have you obeyed the clear command of the Bible to recieve Christ as your Savior? Remember, that's the straightening point. You must *know* the Lord Jesus by following Him in submission and faith.

Second is the test of *walk.* Are you following the Lord in your day-by-day life? The Scripture calls it *abiding* in Christ. Are you being faithful to Him?

Third is the test of *love.* Is there love in your heart for all the brethern? Are you an incourage-ment, not a detriment? Are you part of the solution, or part of the problem? John said, "walk in love."

When you can honestly say that you are making good progress in each of these significant areas of the Christian life, you've *passed the examination!*

1 John 2:12-17

I write unto you, little children, because your sins are forgiven you for His name's sake.

I write unto you, fathers, because ye have known Him that is from the beginning. I write unto you, young men, because ye have overcome the wicked one. I write unto you, little children, because ye have known the Father.

I have written unto you, fathers, because ye have known Him that is from the beginning. I have written unto you, young men, because ye are strong, and the word of God abideth in you, and ye have overcome the wicked one.

Love not the world, neither the things that are in the world. If any man love the world, the love of the Father is not in him.

For all that is in the world, the lust of the flesh, and the lust of the eyes, and the pride of life, is not of the Father, but is of the world.

And the world passeth away, and the lust of it; but he that doeth the will of God abideth forever.

6
All God's Family—and the World

Looking through the family picture album has long been a source of great delight, as well as embarrassment. In these days the photo album has often been replaced by a carousel of slides or a reel of 8-millimeter motion pictures. Regardless of the mode of recording the past, however, the members of the family are captured in different stages of maturity. The apostle John did exactly this when he wrote the "little born ones" in his first epistle. He had the entire family in view when he used the phrase, "I write unto you, little children . . ." (v. 12).

The Greek word *teknia*, translated "little children," appears whenever John addressed the family in the epistle. All of those, but only those, who have the same life in Christ are included. This is the new life given by God that makes one His child.

In the physical realm, one becomes a family member by being born into it. The same is true of the spiritual family. We enter it by being born again. Like produces like; life produces life. The new birth is not produced by dead forms and ceremonies. The "living and powerful" Word of God is the means the Spirit uses to bring about regeneration. James said in his epistle, "Of His own will begot He us *with the word of truth*" (James 1:18). The apostle Paul could say, "For in Christ Jesus I have begotten you *through the gospel*" (1 Corinthians 4:15). And Peter affirmed the same, "Being born again, not of corruptible seed, but of incorruptible, *by the word of God*, which liveth and abideth forever" (1 Peter 1:23).

The living Spirit takes the living Word and performs the miracle of the new birth. By receiving the life from above, we become children of a common Father. Eternal life is the possession of every believer, and that life is divine in character. You recall the purpose of this epistle: "That ye also may have fellowship with us; and truly our fellowship is with the Father, and with His Son, Jesus Christ" (1 John 1:3). Although there may be differing degrees of maturity within the family, the ground of fellowship is the same for all: "Because your sins are forgiven you for His name's sake" (1 John 2:12).

SINS FORGIVEN (v. 12)
All mankind is faced with the question posed by the ancient Job: "How should man be just before God?" (Job 9:2). Man in himself can never answer it to his own or God's satisfaction. The sacrifices of Israel were a divinely appointed way to keep this searching question before

fallen man. Only as we come to the heart realization that "we have redemption through His blood, the forgiveness of sins," do we understand how God "might be just, and the justifier of him who believeth in Jesus" (Romans 3:26).

Yes, the means of our justification comes from the Lord Himself. He made provision by His abundant mercy and rich grace, and we as believers share in the blessing of forgiveness of sins. Through the sacrifice of His Son, the shedding of His blood, the haunting question of Job has been answered once and for all.

FOR HIS NAME'S SAKE
Augustus Toplady wrote, "Not the labor of my hands/ Can fulfill Thy law's demands;/ Could my zeal no respite know,/ Could my tears forever flow,/ All for sin could not atone;/ Thou must save, and Thou alone." You and I as believers in Christ are forgiven for the sake of His blessed name—a name we now bear. Our pardon is based upon divine revelation: "And be ye kind one to another, tenderhearted, forgiving one another, even as God, for Christ's sake, hath forgiven you" (Ephesians 4:32). The angel announced to Joseph, "And she shall bring forth a son, and thou shalt call His name JESUS; for He shall save His people from their sins" (Matthew 1:21). God has forgiven our sin, not because of any merit in us, but because of the infinite merit of the Lord Jesus Christ.

ALL GOD'S FAMILY (vv. 13,14)
Earthly families are composed of parents, young

people, and little children. The same is true in the family of God. The difference, however, is that they do not necessarily vary according to age, but in spiritual maturity. Samuel Rutherford said, "All within the church have not had a like experience of Christ. First John 2:13 makes some fathers, some young men, and some little children. There may be two sons of one and the same father; the one 13 years of age, and the other a nursing child that can neither speak, stand, nor as yet walk." In every assembly of believers, and corporately in the church, there are three distinct stages of spiritual growth. Verses 12 and 13 are addressed to these three classes, and we will examine them separately.

FATHERS

Who were the fathers mentioned in these verses? I believe that John was not referring to men advanced in age, nor those with long standing in the church, though both might qualify. You see, it is possible for people to be well along in years, and even to have been attending the church for decades, and still to be children in knowledge and experience.

Those whom the apostle John addressed as "fathers" no doubt were believers in Christ who themselves had grown in grace and had begotten children in the gospel (1 Corinthians 4:15). By experience, they were the leaders of the little flocks of Christians. They were spiritually mature, well advanced in all aspects of the Christian faith. John referred to them as having "known Him that is from the beginning." F. W.

Grant suggests, "Notice that there are no 'old men' here. No feebleness or decay is hinted at; none at all."

The "fathers" John addressed, therefore, were believers who had a permanent, personal experience with the Lord. Their maturity was marked by their knowledge of Christ. Their lives were centered in a Person; they were occupied with Him. They were like Paul, who said,

> Yea doubtless, and I count all things but loss for the excellency of the knowledge of Christ Jesus, my Lord; for whom I have suffered the loss of all things, and do count them but refuse, that I may win Christ,
>
> And be found in Him, not having mine own righteousness, which is of the law, but that which is through the faith of Christ, the righteousness which is of God by faith;
>
> That I may know Him, and the power of His resurrection, and the fellowship of His sufferings, being made conformable unto His death (Philippians 3:8-10).

What distinguishes the mature Christian? Not how many years he has been a child of God, but the growth and maturity he has achieved in the knowledge of God through Jesus Christ! All too many of God's people are preoccupied with what they receive from the hand of a bountiful Father, but they are not saturated with the knowledge of Him, in Himself and for Himself, apart from His gifts. A.W. Tozer set the standard in his book *The Pursuit of God:* "As we begin to focus upon God, the things of the Spirit will take shape before our inner eyes. . . . A new

God-consciousness will seize upon us and we shall begin to taste and hear and inwardly feel God, who is our life and our all."

YOUNG MEN

This is the designation John gave to Christians who had grown in Christ to the place where they were experiencing victory over the attacks of Satan, the wicked one (v. 13). Peter warned us, "Be sober, be vigilant, because your adversary, the devil, like a roaring lion walketh about, seeking whom he may devour; whom resist steadfast in the faith . . ." (1 Peter 5:8,9). The Bible never tells us to run from the devil. True, we are told to "flee fornication" (1 Corinthians 6:18); we are commanded to "flee youthful lusts" (2 Timothy 2:22). But different instructions are given about our confrontation with the devil! The apostle James declared, "Submit yourselves, therefore, to God. Resist the devil, and he will flee from you" (James 4:7).

What does John have to say about the "young men" in this spiritual family? "I have written unto you, young men, because ye are strong" (v. 14). The word "strong" means "to be powerful" or "to be able." Christian friend, what is the measure of your spiritual strength? How would the apostle, or even the Lord, rate your ability to combat the enemy? Those addressed as "young men" were Christians who had progressed beyond the infant stage in spiritual growth, but who had not yet attained the status indicated by "fathers." They were characterized by power, energy, and ability.

How did they get their strength? It came by continual communion with God. Note the words, "The word of God abideth in you." This inner source of strength is sufficient to escape Satan's wiles and break his power. Knowing and meditating upon the truths of the Bible is the secret of "overcoming the wicked one." There is no other way to do it! In his classic passage on the armor of God, Paul instructed us to take "the sword of the Spirit, which is the word of God" (Ephesians 6:17).

Our conflict with Satan is *real*. The devil is a living person. The sword of the Spirit is the Christian's only weapon of offense against him. But more is needed than simply the quoting of texts. The Word of God must abide in us. This means that our entire life—mind, heart, and spirit—is to be occupied with the Word. When it lives within, it gives us spiritual muscle.

Notice the ring of triumphant victory in John's reference to the conflict with Satan: "Ye *have* overcome the wicked one." The recipients of this letter had been children at first, only knowing the Father. Now, having used the Word and become strong, they were faced with the adversary. As Robert Candlish wrote, "The vigor of spiritual youth points to the never-ending conflict between the seed of the woman and the seed of the serpent. . . . For you are called to wage war with the wicked one. And you have every encouragement to do so. You have overcome him already in Christ, for He has overcome him. You have but to follow up and follow out the conquest. You are strong, and the Word of God abideth in you."

LITTLE CHILDREN

The third class of individuals in the family of God is the "infants." The word "little children" in the authorized version is *paidia* which identifies these believers as newborn babes. They have only recently been born again. They have just come into the family. Nevertheless, John says that they "have known the Father." Our Lord said in His high priestly prayer, "And this is life eternal, that they might know Thee, the only true God, and Jesus Christ, whom Thou hast sent" (John 17:3). How wonderful! They may be immature, but they have the same Father. His name has been manifested to them by the Son. "God hath sent forth the Spirit of His Son into your hearts, crying, Abba, Father" (Galatians 4:6).

In verses 12 through 14 of 1 John 2, the apostle addressed all of God's family. What is your classification within that family? If you are an "infant," only recently born into the family, thank God today that you know the Father. Yours is the opportunity for growth in grace and in the knowledge of the Lord Jesus. If a "young man," press on toward maturity. If a "father," feed the flock of God.

THE FAMILY AND THE WORLD (vv. 15-17)

It appears that these verses are addressed particularly to the "young men." The Word of God abides in them, and they are strong. They had been children, knowing the Father. Now, having used the Word and become strong, they face another adversary—the world, ruled over by the wicked one.

Though these verses apply particularly to the young men in the family of God, they are indeed applicable to every one. The voice of the Holy Spirit warns, "Love not the world, neither the things that are in the world" (v. 15).

What is "the world"? The Greek word for "world" in the New Testament, *kosmos*, has several meanings. Sometimes it refers to the material universe (Romans 1:20). In John 3:16 the word *kosmos* means the human race, or mankind. But the word is found to have an entirely different sense in John 12:31, where our Lord said, "Now is the judgment of this *world*; now shall the prince of this *world* be cast out." The apostle John used this term again in 1 John 5:19, "And we know that we are of God, and the whole *world* lieth in wickedness." Therefore, when the children of God are commanded in the Bible to "love not the world, neither the things that are in the world," the reference is not to the world of persons, but rather to the *world system*. And, this system is characterized and controlled by the principles of Satan.

In the context of this chapter, the family of God is instructed to observe both a positive and a negative principle. The positive, "love one another," is expressed in verses 9 through 11. The negative is proposed in verses 15-17, "Love not the world, neither the things that are in the world." Remember, "God is light" (1 John 1:5). This light reveals the world for exactly what it is—a system presided over by Satan, and which includes everything opposed and contrary to God and His Word.

The love of the Father and the love of the

world are in sharp opposition. As believers, we are part of a supernatural system of which the Father is the source and Christ is the center. But another system appeals to the old nature—the world system. You and I must live in it, find our occupation in it, but yet have nothing to do with it. This world, so violently opposed to Christ, is able to attract the heart and entice us into the way of darkness. This may happen to any child in God's family. Our Lord said in John 17 that He has taken us out of the world. Even though separated from the world, however, we are sent back into it. We have the opportunity and responsibility of displaying the life of Heaven's Sovereign to a system that has as its prince the "accuser of the brethren," the antagonist of Christ.

THE WORLD SYSTEM DESCRIBED

The elements that characterize this world system are set forth in verse 16. By what is it known? "The lust of the flesh, and the lust of the eyes, and the pride of life."

"The lust of the flesh" is the appetite of the senses thrown out of order, out of control. The world's aim is to pervert these appetites, and in so doing they become the lusts of the flesh. We are constantly surrounded by all of the pressures of this world in a direct appeal to the senses, and it becomes so easy to partake of the world's fascinating cup of sinful pleasures. In fact, even the lawful gratification of the body's natural cravings can sometimes get out of control. Yes, the lust of the flesh characterizes the world system.

The "lust of the eyes" is also a powerful source of temptation and expresses itself in the sin of covetousness. It entices us to grasp for visible things like gold, silver, houses, lands, and possessions. This too is of the world.

The "pride of life" is self-centeredness, the constant seeking of praise. Candlish calls it "a game of diplomacy and a race of emulation. . . . It puts the men and women of the world on a poor struggle to outmaneuver and outshine one another, to outdo one another—for the most part in mere externals."

To review, the appeal of the world is described in a threefold way—the lust of the flesh, the lust of the eyes, and the pride of life. Was this not the original temptation of the woman in Eden? She saw that the tree was "good for food"—the lust of the flesh. She experienced that the tree was "pleasant to the eyes"—the lust of the eyes. She also saw that it was "a tree to be desired to make one wise"—the pride of life.

Our Lord was confronted with this same threefold temptation in the wilderness. The prince of this world, Satan, sought to get the perfect Christ to yield to temptation. But our Lord met him with the Word of God, which was abiding in Him and with which He overcame the wicked one. Only by obedience to God and His Word can the Christian remain free from the degrading influences of the world system that surrounds us.

How shall we break away from the appetite for worldly things? How may worldly Christians become the unworldly Christians we should be?

The Scripture answers us, "This is the victory that overcometh the world, *even our faith*" (1 John 5:4). While we remain in our earthly bodies, we are still in this world; but if we have been born of God, we are "not of the world." Whenever we then find ourselves being over-come—that the world is encroaching upon our hearts, our time, our strength—let us remember that we are not of this world, but another. Our "citizenship is in heaven" (Philippians 3:20). Let us serve its King.

THE WORLD WILL PASS AWAY

Satan's system is destined to ruin. He is the prince of a temporary kingdom, and one day even our desire for it will be taken away. "And the world passeth away, and the lust of it" (1 John 2:17). The world and its entire system will be overthrown, and every desire for it will also be gone.

Child of God, make double sure—whether "father," "young man," or "little child"—that your interests are not centered in any way upon that which will pass away. John said, "He that doeth the will of God abideth forever" (v. 17). How we need this exhortation: "Wherefore, receiving a kingdom which cannot be moved, let us have grace, by which we may serve God acceptably with reverence and godly fear"! (Hebrews 12:28).

WHAT ABOUT YOU?

In response to the apostle's clear and powerful description of the world system and the Christian's warfare, I suggest that you engage in a few moments of spiritual introspection. Ask yourself the three questions indicated in the verses we have studied. Be honest. If changes are needed, ask God to help you effect them.

What is my attitude toward:
1. The will of God as revealed in His Word? (2:3-5).
2. The children of God? (2:9-11).
3. The world? (2:15-17).

1 John 2:18-23,27,28

Little children, it is the last time; and as ye have heard that antichrist shall come, even now are there many antichrists, by which we know that it is the last time.

They went out from us, but they were not of us; for if they had been of us, they would no doubt have continued with us; but they went out, that they might be made manifest that they were not all of us.

But ye have an unction from the Holy One, and ye know all things.

I have not written unto you because ye know not the truth, but because ye know it, and that no lie is of the truth.

Who is a liar but he that denieth that Jesus is the Christ? He is antichrist, that denieth the Father and the Son.

Whosoever denieth the Son, the same hath not the Father; he that confesseth the Son hath the Father also.

But the anointing which ye have received of Him abideth in you, and ye need not that any man teach you; but as the same anointing teacheth you of all things, and is truth, and is no lie, and even as it hath taught you, ye shall abide in Him.

And now, little children, abide in Him, that, when He shall appear, we may have confidence and not be ashamed before Him at His coming.

7

Fatherly Advice

Among my boyhood memories is a time when my father sat me down in the wicker chair on the back porch and proceeded to warn me about certain boys who lived in our neighborhood. His concern for my moral welfare had always clearly emphasized what was right; now he was giving me strict orders about what was wrong. In the portion of Scripture before us, the apostle writing under inspiration of the Holy Spirit did exactly that for the members of the family of God.

John had just finished making a sharp contrast between God and the world (vv. 15-17). He indicated that the Christian is confronted by many dangerous foes. One of these is the world, with its tendency to press the believer into its satanic mold. John's injunction was definite: "Love not the world, neither the things that are in the world" (v. 15).

Now he speaks of another danger, perhaps

more treacherous than the world itself—false teaching. Why is it so dangerous? Because Satan operates primarily in the realm of religion. He knows that people are prone to be enticed and misled by that which is novel and different. He delights in deceiving with new ideas, or by twisting the truth, or by outright apostasy.

THE WARNING (vv. 18,19)

The apostle's attention turns once more to the "little children." Their position in the family was one of spiritual infancy, or they had recently been born again. Because of their spiritual immaturity, they were in special need of a warning about false teaching.

John informed those new Christians that they were living in "the last time" (v. 18). That era has already continued for nineteen centuries, so we are living in "the last time" today as well. No new age has begun since the Holy Spirit came down at Pentecost. We are beyond the cross. We are beyond the ascension. We are in that period of time known as the "end of the age." We are awaiting Christ's return. Peter wrote,

> But, beloved, be not ignorant of this one thing, that one day is with the Lord as a thousand years, and a thousand years as one day.
>
> The Lord is not slack concerning His promise, as some men count slackness, but is longsuffering toward us, not willing that any should perish, but that all should come to repentance (2 Peter 3:8,9).

Under God's patient loving kindness and grace, this "last time" will continue until He has brought all of the redeemed safely to Himself. The completed body of Christ will then be raptured. John then repeats the same warning given by the apostle Paul to the Thessalonian believers, "For the mystery of iniquity doth already work" (2 Thessalonians 2:7), for he says, "Even now are there many antichrists." This in itself was proof that he was writing in the last time, the last hour, for antichrists were already at work in the world. The Antichrist himself will not be revealed until after the translation of the church (2 Thessalonians 2:8).

"Anti" means "instead of." An antichrist therefore is a false or spurious christ. "Anti" also means "in opposition to." So an antichrist is one who is hostile to Christ. Error has always presented itself in the guise of truth, even though opposed to it. This is in keeping with the method of that final counterfeit to be foisted upon the world by Satan—the supreme Antichrist (see 2 Thessalonians 2:4). He will first present himself as God; then he will reveal his opposition to the Lord of Glory. This pattern is true of all apostate religions and their leaders. First they present themselves as substitutes for the true; then they show their real colors in absolute opposition to the truth.

How up to date this warning is! Reading these words of the apostle John is like reading about the present-day church. These enemies of Christ had professed the faith, but something was wrong. John said, "They went out from us." The Scofield notes suggest that this was a doctrinal departure. Perhaps it was both doctrinal *and* geographical, and they literally left the fellowship to start a group of their own. Peter gave a graphic description of this kind of false teacher in his second epistle (2 Peter 2:19-22), which serves as a stern reminder that not all who profess Christ are actually believers. Some are antichrists, out to deceive and destroy.

Note that John said they went out "from *us.*" This pronoun is used five times in verse 19, underscoring the wonderful fellowship that marked the early believers. John had written, "That which we have seen and heard declare we unto you, that ye also may have fellowship with us; and truly our fellowship is with the Father, and with His Son, Jesus Christ" (1 John 1:3). By departing, these enemies of the gospel had indicated that they were not of the "us," the body. They had never been part of that mystical union of Christ and believers, so the apostle John said finally, "They were not of us."

This was a case of deliberate apostasy. After professing to be Christians, they promoted a false doctrine and sought to mislead God's people. Paul described counterfeits like them as follows: ". . . as Jannes and Jambres withstood Moses, so do these also resist the truth, men of corrupt minds, reprobate concerning the faith. But they shall proceed no further; for their folly shall be manifest unto all men, as theirs also was" (2 Timothy 3:8,9). They left the assembly of believers, the fellowship of Christ's followers. By so doing, they revealed themselves for what they actually were—opposers of Christ.

OUR PROTECTION (v. 20)

Our attention is turned from the unreal, the counterfeit, by the use of the happy conjunction, *"but ye."* The writer stated a proposition that is true of every believer: regardless of your position in the body, of your maturity or lack of it in Christian doctrine, of your gifts small or large, you "have an unction from the Holy One, and ye know all things" (see v. 20). Keep in mind that John was speaking to the little children, the relatively new believers. Even they possessed this gift from on high.

The words "unction" in verse 20 and "anointing" in verse 27 come from the same Greek term. What is this unction, this anointing? It is a person—the Holy Spirit. "By this know we that we dwell in Him, and He in us, because He hath given us of His Spirit" (1 John 4:13). W. E. Vine wrote, "The passage teaches that the gift of the Holy Spirit is the all-efficient means of enabling believers to possess a knowledge of the truth."

The Lord Jesus was called the *christos*, the "anointed one." The Holy Spirit is the *chrisma*, the "anointing." One of His primary functions as our indweller is to lead us into the truth and thereby to keep us safe from error.

Our Lord made this promise, "Nevertheless, when He, the Spirit of truth, is come, He will guide you into all truth" (John 16:13). The Spirit was given as our instructor. "All things" are revealed by Him, and they comprise the "all truth" promised by Christ. Think of it! We have an infallible teacher—the Holy Spirit Himself!

John certainly did not mean to imply that

these believers had anything resembling perfect knowledge. But because they had received the anointing of the Holy One, of the Spirit of God abiding within them, they had the capacity to judge all things presented to them. Because they were led by Him, they knew the truth. This was exactly what the apostle Paul had said to the believers at Corinth;

Which things also we speak, not in the words which man's wisdom teacheth, but which the Holy Spirit teacheth, comparing spiritual things with spiritual.

But the natural man receiveth not the things of the Spirit of God; for they are foolishness unto him, neither can he know them, because they are spiritually discerned.

But he that is spiritual judgeth all things, yet he himself is judged of no man.

For who hath known the mind of the Lord, that he may instruct Him? But we have the mind of Christ (1 Corinthians 2:13-16).

Spiritual perception comes only from the indwelling Holy Spirit. We therefore have two divine safeguards—the Holy Spirit and the Word. The Spirit dwells in our hearts and we hold the Scriptures in our hands. This, of course, is not to exclude the ministry of the God-appointed and gifted teachers of the Word spoken of in Ephesians 4:11. But in the final analysis our knowledge comes through the applying of the truth of the Bible by the Holy Spirit.

Many adverse winds of doctrine blow today.

Many voices clamor for a hearing—some true, some false. Personal experiences are being highly touted among professing believers as the way to know the truth. I've even heard of people saying, "I don't care what the Bible says. I know what happened to me, and that's all that counts."

But, friend, experience and Scripture *must coincide.* The Spirit of God never contradicts the Word of God. He cannot do so, because He is the author of the Bible. Therefore, if your experience is not in accord with the Word of God, *it is wrong!* The Holy Spirit faithfully reveals the Word of God to our hearts, and all that contradicts it is in error.

Griffith Thomas has suggested that if we have an "unction from the Holy One," then we ought to distrust even our own intellectual powers and reasonings in spiritual matters. We should be especially wary of counsel about spiritual truths received from people who are not born again. Finally, we should be fully led and controlled by the Word of God through the Spirit of God. This will give us perfect guidance.

Aaron the high priest was anointed with oil before he could perform his duties. At His baptism, the Lord Jesus was anointed by the Spirit. Then, after His death, resurrection, and ascension, He brought His disciples into fellowship with Himself by the impartation of the Spirit. Jesus was anointed "with the oil of gladness" above His fellows (Hebrews 1:9). That same Holy Spirit, the One who anointed Jesus as the Holy One of God, now dwells in His mystical body, the church. He abides in the heart of every believer. "Now if any man have not the Spirit of Christ, he is none of His" (Romans 8:9). Yes, we have an unction from on High. The Spirit within gives us the capacity to recognize the truths of God. This in turn protects us from the influence and errors of the false christs.

A COMFORTING WORD (v. 21)
What encouragement the apostle now gives to these little children! He was not writing them because of their ignorance, for they had been furnished with divine equipment that caused them to "know all things." Rather, he wrote to show the relationship of this knowledge to their conduct. What had happened? Some had left them doctrinally, perhaps also literally leaving the church. There was therefore a distinct possibility that these little ones might be disturbed; that their growth might be jeopardized. So the apostle reminded them of three important facts:

1. *They had the truth.* "Because ye know it," he said. They knew the Father, who is the God of truth. They had believed in Christ, who is "the way, the truth, and the life." They were indwelt by the Holy Spirit, who is called the Spirit of truth.

2. *Lies and the truth cannot be interchanged.* "No lie is of the truth." When I recently had to replace some tubes in an old radio, I discovered that some of them were no longer available. The salesman in the radio shop consulted a chart and found which tubes could be substituted for

the discontinued, defective ones. Not so in God's shop! Spiritual truth is uncompromising. God allows no substitutes. "No lie is of the truth."

3. *The lie and the liar are of common cloth.* The spirit of falsehood quickly betrays its true character. Eventually, not only the perversion of the truth but also the purveyor of the lie will be brought out into the open.

PINPOINTING THE LIAR (vv. 22,23)

"Who is a liar but he that denieth that Jesus is the Christ? He is antichrist, that denieth the Father and the Son." Indeed, distortion and denial of the truth have always marked those who have the spirit of antichrist—who are part of the "mystery of iniquity" already at work today. Down through the ages of church history, they have always been active in promoting the spiritual lie.

The apostle now proceeds to tell us how to identify apostates, false teachers, and promoters of the spirit of antichrist. First we are to determine the relationship of every teacher and doctrine to the person and work of our Lord Jesus Christ. This will tell whether it is of antichrist or not. The outstanding distinguishing mark of the system of Satan is its denial of the person of Christ. The deity and humanity of the Lord Jesus is the central point of controversy.

To deny that Jesus is the Christ is to deny the fullness of His work as the Messiah. Griffith Thomas reminds us that this includes His ministry as prophet, priest, and king. As prophet, Christ was the anointed One, making Himself responsible for the Scriptures. As prophet, He was the revealer of God, for "He hath declared Him" (John 1:18). As prophet, He was the faithful witness (Revelation 1:5; 3:14). And as prophet He declared, "But take heed; behold, I have *foretold* you all things" (Mark 13:23).

The anointed One is not only God's prophet, He is also His priest. He is called our "Great High Priest" (Hebrews 4:14,15). As priest, He had something to offer (Hebrews 9:28). As priest, He intercedes on behalf of His people (Hebrews 3:1). And as priest, He is able to sustain and bring comfort (Hebrews 2:17,18).

Included as well in the term "messiah" is the glorious truth that He performs the office of king. In Revelation 15:3, Christ is called the "King," even though the time of His coronation has not yet come. His sacrifice complete, He sits at God's right hand, "From henceforth expecting till His enemies be made His footstool" (Hebrews 10:13). One day He will return in power and great glory. He will subdue this rebellious earth and reign as its rightful king.

But with righteousness shall He judge the poor, and reprove with equity for the meek of the earth; and He shall smite the earth with the rod of His mouth, and with the breath of His lips shall He slay the wicked.

And righteousness shall be the girdle of His loins, and faithfulness the girdle of His waist (Isaiah 11:4,5).

The work of Jesus Christ is inseparable from His

person. In fact, His work is dependent upon His deity. All who acknowledge Him as Lord also recognize His redemptive activities. False teachers and apostates, those who have the spirit of antichrist, deny His incarnation and His sacrificial death for sin. They mock at His virgin birth. And, they refuse to acknowledge His deity.

The acid test is really that same question Jesus asked about Himself in Caesarea Philippi, "Who do men say that I, the Son of man, am?" (Matthew 16:13). Peter's response to this telling question was, "Thou art the Christ, the Son of the living God" (v. 16). Men may say that they know the Father. They may even speak of "the universal Fatherhood of God," yet all the while denying that Jesus is the Christ. The apostle tells us that all who deny the Son *do not have* the Father. This forever settles the question about whether or not Unitarians can be called Christians. Absolutely not!

As I recently rode down the boulevard of a large city in America, I passed a church known around the world. It has been the center of social action; its pulpit has been filled primarily by men who deny the deity of Jesus Christ. And yet that church is still labeled "Christian." I said to myself, "Not so!"

Some believe that Christ was simply a great teacher or even a specially created being, but they deny that He is the Son of God. They are of antichrist! They do not have the Father, because whoever denies the Son "hath not the Father." The Son is the revelation of the Father, and the Lord Jesus said, "No man cometh unto the Father, but by Me" (John 14:6). He further declared, "He that hath seen Me hath seen the Father" (John 14:9). In John 10:30 He added, "I and My Father are one." Fellowship with God the Father and His Son, Jesus Christ, is not possible to anyone who rejects the Son. A denial that Jesus Christ was God manifest in the flesh is the work of the spirit of antichrist, and negates all possibility of fellowship.

A REMINDER (vv. 27,28)
The apostle concluded this passage by reiterating the fact (a fact especially strengthening to young believers) that the anointing we have received of Christ (that is, the Holy Spirit) abides in us. Prior to His ascension the Lord Jesus promised His disciples, "And I will pray the Father, and He shall give you another Comforter, that He may abide with you forever" (John 14:16). Of this One the Lord Jesus said, "He shall teach you all things, and bring all things to your remembrance, whatever I have said unto you" (John 14:26). The truth we receive is authenticated by the indwelling Spirit.

Believer's Responsibility
Every believer has the solemn responsibility to abide in Christ (vv. 27,28). These words are in the imperative mood in both verses; they are commands. The result of abiding in Him is spiritual fruit.

Believer's Reward
When we accept this responsibility, we can expect a reward at His coming. "That, when He

shall appear, we may have confidence and not be ashamed before Him at His coming" (v. 28). That word "confidence" is translated elsewhere "boldness," and means "freedom of speech" or "the absence of the fear which accompanies frank expression." How wonderful that this can be true of us when we see our Lord! It will be a time of reward, and we'll "not be ashamed before Him!"

I believe that another factor may also be involved in verse 28. The apostle John may be making a strong plea for believers to abide in Christ so that when the Lord Jesus appears, He Himself will have confidence and not be ashamed of us before the Father. Surely, the deep desire of every minister of the gospel, every pastor of the flock, is that the sheep in his care will abide in Christ and be faithful. What joy will ring out in the heart of the faithful undershepherd when the Chief Shepherd appears and finds the sheep abiding in Him! The apostle Paul said, "For what is our hope, or joy, or crown of rejoicing? Are not even *ye* in the presence of our Lord Jesus Christ at His coming?" (1 Thessalonians 2:19). Every faithful minister will have this same expectation, this earnest desire.

Dear Christian, *abide* in Christ. Allow the blessed Holy Spirit to fill and control you. Let the very life of the Lord Jesus produce fruit through you to His glory. Then you and those who have ministered to you will rejoice in the day of Christ's coming!

1 John 2:29-3:1-3

If ye know that He is righteous, ye know that everyone that doeth righteousness is born of Him.

Behold, what manner of love the Father hath bestowed upon us, that we should be called the children of God; therefore, the world knoweth us not, because it knew Him not.

Beloved, now are we the children of God, and it doth not yet appear what we shall be, but we know that, when He shall appear, we shall be like Him; for we shall see Him as He is.

And every man that hath this hope in him purifieth himself even as He is pure.

8

O Glorious Calling!

The dominant theme of the gospel of John is eternal life in Jesus Christ. The dominant theme in the first epistle is this same eternal life in the believer. The nature of a father should be found in his offspring; the Divine nature must necessarily be in the children of God. The idea of sonship runs throughout this letter, particularly in this section.

The epistle may be outlined as follows:
1. God is light (1:5-2:28).
2. God is righteous (2:29-4:6).
3. God is love (4:7-5:21).

Corresponding to these three divisions are three tests of the Christian life:
1. Believing in Christ (1:5-2:28).
2. Doing righteousness (2:29-4:6).
3. Loving one another (4:7-5:21).

We turn now to the second major division of John's epistle: God is righteous. We who are His children are to walk in righteousness.

99

A REQUIRED IDENTIFICATION (v. 29)

A driver's license or credit card may do for identification when you cash a check at the department store. But a name on a church membership roll or a gold cross on a chain around your neck or a headful of biblical knowledge does not necessarily identify you as a child of God. Please. We must not evade this important point. If we do, we will encounter a difficulty that may affect us for all eternity.

John wrote, "If ye know that He is righteous, ye know that everyone that doeth righteousness is born of Him" (1 John 2:29). The apostle previously had spoken of our fellowship "with the Father, and with His Son, Jesus Christ." This is a fellowship of light, based upon knowledge and belief. Now his attention shifts to a new kind of fellowship—the fellowship of righteousness. God is not only light, He is also righteous. All who claim to be the children of the Heavenly Father are of the same nature. Therefore, begotten of Him, they live in righteousness. This holy walk is positive identification that they are born of God. And, if one is truly born again by faith in Christ, John says he will possess the following qualities:

1. *A righteousness not natural to man (v. 29).* God is righteous in His very character. It is impossible for the sons of Adam to produce the same righteousness which is inherent to the nature of God. Jesus declared to Nicodemus, "That which is born of the flesh is flesh" (John 3:6). On another occasion He said to a group of religious leaders, "If ye were Abraham's children, ye would do the works of Abraham"

(John 8:39). The character of a father is demonstrated in his child. If that quality is missing, one must question the relationship. Just so, the natural man cannot please God. "There is none righteous, no, not one" (Romans 3:10).

2. *Knowledge*. John said that we can *"know that He is righteous"* (v. 29). The children of God possess a knowledge of God's holiness. I believe this refers to the Father, because we are "born of Him." You may disagree, feeling that the clause refers specifically to the Lord Jesus. I would not argue with you, for we do know Christ as "the righteous One." Not only do we know that He is righteous, we also are aware that "everyone that doeth righteousness" is born of God (v. 29).

3. *Life*. A tree can only produce fruit of its own kind. As God is righteous, so all who receive His life will live in righteousness. Please take careful note! Regardless of any profession of faith that may appear to be genuine, regardless of any emotional experience that purports to be real, regardless of any religious activity that seems to be authentic, only the men and women who *practice* righteousness are "born of God." Holiness of walk will be their way of life. "Can the fig tree, my brethren, bear olive berries? Either a vine, figs?" (James 3:12). Make no mistake! All who are truly born of God will manifest a righteousness that can be produced by the divine nature.

We do not and cannot live righteously so that we can become the children of God. It's the other way around. Those who have received the new life by faith will demonstrate that newness of life by the way they live. The identifying mark of the new nature in the heart is righteous living in the world.

A PRESENT RELATIONSHIP (3:1)

Chapter 3 begins with an exclamation of wonderment that we should be called God's children. John immediately added, "Beloved, now are we the children of God" (v. 2). I detect a note of amazement here. John had just spoken of being born of God. Now he presents his heart reaction to this wonderful truth. An expanded translation of this clause might read, "See what an incredible quality of love the Father has given us!"

What a privilege to receive this divine gift! Man's love might change conditions, alter circumstances, or render assistance in a time of need. But God's love gives us a new nature. It makes us His child. This was a past transaction—and is a present reality.

In verse 2 the emphasis is placed upon the present. "*Now* are we the children of God." This was not always the case. Those who say we are born into this world the children of God are in error. We were not so by creation; we *become* so by the new creation. We were not His children by the flesh, because "that which is born of the flesh is flesh" (John 3:6). Rather, we are children of God "by faith in Jesus Christ." It's not by generation, but by the regeneration of the Holy Spirit.

But as many as received Him, to them gave
He power to become the children of God,
even to them that believe on His name;

Who were born, not of blood, nor of the
will of the flesh, nor of the will of man, but
of God (John 1:12,13).

And Paul said, "Therefore, if any man be in
Christ, he is a new creation" (2 Corinthians
5:17).

I have occasionally asked someone, "Are you
a Christian?" The reply was, "Oh yes, I have always been one." It can't be! John negates this
expression of human pride and presumption by
saying, *'Now* are we the children of God."
Once we were strangers, aliens, enemies of God
(see Romans 5). We were without hope and
without God in the world. But now are we
God's own! What amazing grace that the lost
and guilty, having no claim upon God, should
become recipients of His divine nature.

John's selection of the word "children" implies a birth. We are born again and given a new
nature. My friend, divine love is God's grace in-
action. It's undeserved. With no assurance or
possibility of its being returned, God in love has
drawn us to Himself. George Williams said,
"With God, 'to call' is to cause to be sons." The
pathway of God's sovereign grace is this:

For whom He did foreknow, He also did
predestinate to be conformed to the image
of His Son, that He might be the firstborn
among many brethren.

Moreover, whom He did predestinate,
them He also called; and whom He called,
them He also justified; and whom He
justified, them He also glorified (Romans
8:29,30).

The hymnwriter exulted in this marvelous truth

and exclaimed, "Children of God, O glorious calling!"

Do you think unbelievers like to admit that Christians are members of God's family? Certainly not! They refuse to acknowledge that we are the children of God, just as they do not recognize or acknowledge that Christ is the Son of God. Why? Because spiritual things are spiritually discerned: "But the natural man receiveth not the things of the Spirit of God; for they are foolishness unto Him, neither can he know them, because they are spiritually discerned" (1 Corinthians 2:14).

The apostle Paul said that "the world by wisdom *knew not God*" (1 Corinthians 1:21). The Lord Jesus declared to the men of His day, leaders in their religion, "Ye neither know Me, nor My Father; if ye had known Me, ye should have known My Father also" (John 8:19). The people of this world system are not of the Father, and therefore the child of God should expect that they will not know him. It's exactly as the Lord Jesus said, "If the world hate you, ye know that it hated Me before it hated you. If ye were of the world, the world would love its own; but because ye are not of the world, but I have chosen you out of the world, therefore the world hateth you" (John 15:18,19).

Robert Candlish wrote, "Let us lay our account with having to judge and act on principles which the world cannot understand. Let us be God's children indeed; though on that very account the world that has not known God should not know us."

A RESERVATION IN HEAVEN (v. 2)

But the current role of believers in the world is not permanent: ". . . it doth not yet appear what we shall be" (v. 2). The glory of God is to reveal; it is also His glory to conceal. Right now, Christians seem to be like all others in outward appearance. Two people walking side by side, pushed back and forth by a great crowd, are not distinguishable as to their spiritual condition. One may be a godly Christian with the hope of the resurrection "out from among the dead," and the other an unregenerated sinner awaiting the "resurrection unto damnation." Someone has said, "The pilgrims of faith passing through the world wear but humble garb. Like their Lord, they are wayfarers on earth." Nothing of Jesus' appearance betrayed His kingly nature. Passing through this world, we too do not look like royalty. But we are! "Now are we the children of God!"

Quite often King James V of Scotland would roam among his subjects in disguise. On one such journey through the Highlands, he came with a friend to an inn. He sat at the common dining table and ate with the other travelers. As he and his companion went upstairs to their room, a man who had sat at the table questioned the innkeeper. "Who is the taller of those two men gone upstairs?" The innkeeper replied, "Farmer John of Ballengeuch." "Farmer nothing," the man excitedly whispered. "I know him. My eyes deceive me not, he is Royal James." God's children are like Scotland's king at the inn. We are for the present disguised, but our heritage will one day be known.

God could have taken us on to Glory the moment He saved us. But He left us here to live among men. It has pleased Him to keep us in our physical bodies so that we might testify of our living Lord and a salvation completely of grace. Yes, we who have "the firstfruits of the Spirit" still "groan within ourselves, waiting for the adoption, that is, the redemption of our body" (Romans 8:23). I have heard "groaning" saints say, "Why doesn't God take me Home?" Friend, if you are homesick for glory—perhaps questioning the trial you are now passing through—take comfort in the truth that God is not through with you yet. "It doth not yet appear what we shall be." Remembering that God reserves some secrets to Himself, trust Him for the present. A great day of glorification is coming.

OUR FUTURE GLORY (v. 2)

Not only are believers in Christ privileged to be part of God's family now, we are heirs of a future glory as well. "But we know that, when He shall appear, we shall be like Him; for we shall see Him as He is" (v. 2). At present we are in disguise, but the day is coming when the full rights and blessings of membership in God's family will be manifest to all. That which God started in eternity past, when He predestinated us "to be conformed to the image of His Son," will be brought to fruition when Christ appears and "we shall be like Him."

The coming of our Lord will bring to reality all that our hearts and hopes have craved for. "For now we see in a mirror, darkly; but then, face to face; now I know in part, but then shall I know even as also I am known" (1 Corinthians 13:12). That day will be the answer to our Lord's prayer, "Father, I will that they also, whom Thou hast given Me, be with Me where I am, that they may behold My glory . . ." (John 17:24).

Friend, we can well afford to be obscure, despised, and rejected now. We are waiting for His appearance, for the day His glory is fully revealed in us (Romans 8:19; Colossians 3:4). For the child of God, the best is yet to be!

Andrew Bonar sent Spurgeon a copy of his commentary on Leviticus. Spurgeon was so blessed by the exposition that he returned the book with this notation: "Dr. Bonar, please place herein your autograph and photograph." Soon the book was returned with this message from the saintly Bonar. "Dear Spurgeon: Here is the book with my autograph and photograph. If you had been willing to wait a short season, you could have had a better likeness, for I shall be like Him. I shall see Him as He is."

The poet expressed it like this:

> When Christ their life shall be made
> manifest,
> When He shall come with all His power
> to rule,
> Their glory, hidden long, shall be
> confessed;
> Arise and shine! O bright and beautiful!
> With Christ ye shall ascend on high,
> Victorious in His victory.

The apostle Paul wrote, "In a moment, in the twinkling of an eye, at the last trump; for the trumpet shall sound, and the dead shall be raised incorruptible, and we shall be changed" (1 Corinthians 15:52). At that grand moment we will be transformed into Christ's image. Our salvation will reach its culmination. "We shall be like Him!" This is the glorious expectation of the children of God. What more could we hope for? What more could there be? Nothing greater than that! "To be like Him" is to stand in all the perfection that is God. As He was the image of the invisible God, so we shall be the image of Him who is the visible God-man. "Children of God, O glorious calling!"

A CONTINUING OBLIGATION (v. 3)

The child of God looks forward eagerly to seeing the Savior and being like Him. The apostle Paul described our expectation as follows: "Looking for that blessed hope, and the glorious appearing of the great God and our Savior, Jesus Christ" (Titus 2:13). That hope leads us to begin living *now* according to our future glory. Verse 3 of our text may be literally translated, "And everyone having this hope set on Him, purifies himself as that One is pure."

Since we are expecting to be like Christ in Heaven, why not begin right now to live as we will then? The grace of God is operative now within, teaching us that "denying ungodliness and worldly lusts, we should live soberly, righteously, and godly, *in this present age*" (Titus 2:12).

Our hope is set upon seeing Christ and becoming like Him—and our effort should be to live like Him right now. We should not only look to our future glory; we must intensify our effort to please Christ today. When the Lord Jesus Christ comes, He will receive the church unto Himself as "a glorious church, not having spot, or wrinkle, or any such thing; but . . . holy and without blemish" (Ephesians 5:27). Although we know that this pattern of perfection is impossible, we should be striving to reach that ideal. We must say with Paul,

Brethren, I count not myself to have apprehended; but this one thing I do, forgetting those things which are behind, and reaching forth unto those things which are before,

I press toward the mark for the prize of the high calling of God in Christ Jesus (Philippians 3:13, 14).

Alexander Maclaren said of this passage, "My brother, is that your type of Christianity? Is it like the electricity of the northern lights, that paints your winter sky with vanishing, useless splendors of crimson and blue? Or have you got it harnessed to your tram cars, lighting your houses, driving your sewing machines, doing practical work in your daily life?"

Perhaps soon our Lord Jesus will return and we shall be raptured. What glory awaits the children of God! The anticipation of seeing Christ and of being conformed perfectly to His image should daily stir within our hearts and lives a growing sanctification. "Children of God, O glorious calling!"

1 John 3:4-10

Whosoever committeth sin transgresseth also the law; for sin is the transgression of the law.

And ye know that He was manifested to take away our sins, and in Him is no sin.

Whosoever abideth in Him sinneth not; whosoever sinneth hath not seen Him, neither known Him.

Little children, let no man deceive you: he that doeth righteousness is righteous, even as He is righteous.

He that committeth sin is of the devil; for the devil sinneth from the beginning. For this purpose the Son of God was manifested, that He might destroy the works of the devil.

Whosoever is born of God doth not commit sin; for His seed remaineth in him, and he cannot sin, because he is born of God.

In this the children of God are manifest, and the children of the devil: whosoever doeth not righteousness is not of God, neither he that loveth not his brother.

9

A Matter of Lifestyle

This portion of John's epistle is one of the most controversial passages in all of the New Testament. A right interpretation of this Scripture brings great assurance to the heart of the child of God. A wrong interpretation leads to the acceptance of a system of doctrine which contradicts other New Testament teaching. It promotes a quavering uncertainty, an "on again, off again, gone again" salvation for those who endorse it.

Read 1 John 3:4-10 again carefully. These verses confront us with several underlying questions. Do they teach that if a person sins he is not a child of God? Do they say that if a person is a Christian he does not and cannot sin? Just how are we to interpret them?

Before we can understand this passage, we must know the use of Greek verb tenses. In our English language, the tense of a verb relates primarily to time, telling us that the action is past, present, or future. But another factor comes into play in the Greek. Not only does the verb tell the *time* of the action, but it also indicates the *kind* of action.

The present tense verb always denotes a continuous action in present time. For instance, the word "sinneth" in verse 6 is in the present tense, indicating a continuous action. It refers to a person who habitually commits a sin. It tells us that sin is the very lifestyle of that person. In other words, continuous action is the equivalent of our word "practice." The word "sinneth" in verse 6 could therefore be translated "one who practices sin as a habit of life."

THE CONTRAST (vv. 4-6)

John made a sharp distinction between the one who abides in Christ and a person who "hath not seen Him, neither known Him" (v. 6). No middle ground is possible here! If a person abides in Christ, he does not practice sin. But if sin is his way of life, he does not know Christ as his personal Savior. As we look at the verses, several points will be noted.

1. To practice sin is to break the law of God continually (v. 4). The very heart of sin is lawlessness. Literally, verse 4 reads, "Everyone doing sin also does lawlessness, and sin is lawlessness." The important factor here is the will of God! You see, far more is involved than just the transgression of the law. The person who continues sinning refuses to be restrained and regulated by God's commands and His will.

Man is lawless by his very nature. Paul indicated this in Romans 5:13,14. The law had not yet been given in the period of time from Adam to Moses, yet death as the result of sin continued to take its toll. Then, when the law was set down through Moses, its positive commands put man's nature to the test, and his lawlessness soon became evident. Of course, his disobedience had been demonstrated in the garden at the very beginning. Only one thing did God deny man and forbid him to take; yet Satan used this to produce suspicion in Adam's heart, and the fall came.

2. Christ is our example (v. 5). Sin is the expression of man's sinful nature. In all of history, there has been one, and only one, whose nature was free from sin. Christ, the servant of Jehovah, could say, "I do *always* those things that please Him [My Father]" (John 8:29). He also said, "My food is to do the will of Him that sent Me, and to finish His work" (John 4:34). And here John said of Christ, "And ye know that He was manifested to take away our sins, and *in Him is no sin*" (1 John 3:5). The culmination of His work, His death on the cross, was to deal with sin. When John the Baptist saw Him, he cried, "Behold the Lamb of God, who taketh away *the sin* of the world" (John 1:29). Yes, Christ who was Himself sinless was made sin for us so that the problem of the sinful nature could be taken care of.

But that is not all. John also told us that Christ came to earth to "take away *our sins*" (v. 5). Through His death at Calvary He took care of both the root and the fruit. He became the sin offering for *what we are* by nature, and the trespass offering for *what we do* because of that sin nature. By His own sinlessness, He gave us the example of what our lives should be.

3. A believer does not practice sin (v. 6). "Whosoever abideth in Him sinneth not; whosoever sinneth hath not seen Him, neither known Him." This expresses the contrast between one who abides in Christ and one who has not come to Him in faith. It's as simple as this: If a person abides in Christ, he will not sin; if he sins, he does not know Him as Savior.

A real danger confronted the believers of John's day, and it threatens us as well. Some Christians were saying that conduct doesn't matter; that whether you sin or not makes no difference. No doubt one of the reasons John wrote his epistle was to correct this error, for he said, "These things have I written unto you concerning them that seduce you" (1 John 2:26).

But some people go to the other extreme, teaching that if a person commits a single sin, he is no longer a child of God. Clearly, this position is also incorrect, for John said,

My little children, these things write I unto you, that ye sin not. And if any man sin, we have an advocate with the Father, Jesus Christ the righteous (1 John 2:1).

John was aware, as we are, that Christians will occasionally sin. The high and holy standard of God is that we "sin not." The believer's lifestyle is *not* characterized by sinning. He may disobey, fail, and sin; but this is not the manner of his life in Christ. The one who is abiding in Christ does not habitually practice sin.

Diametrically opposed to this is the style of life of one who sins continually, who lives in

constant disobedience. This person has not seen
or known the Lord Jesus; he has never beheld
Him with the eye of faith. He has never seen
the glory, beauty, and fullness of Christ, nor
His ability to meet his need. On the basis of this
inspired text, we may say that he does not
know Christ as His Savior.

How different is the child of God! The apostle
Paul declared, "But we all, with unveiled face be-
holding as in a mirror the glory of the Lord, are
changed into the same image from glory to glory,
even as by the Spirit of the Lord" (2 Corinthians
3:18). Unlike those who practice sin, who have
not known the Savior, the Christian "beholds"
the glory of the Lord and is transformed more
and more into His likeness.

CENTRAL CERTAINTIES (vv. 7,8)
The child of God will develop a pattern of behavior that results from a right relationship with
God. John is determined to keep his "little
children" from being deceived or led astray. The
apostle Paul said, "Be not deceived, God is not
mocked, for whatever a man soweth, that shall
he also reap" (Galatians 6:7). A similar warning
is contained in these words: "Know ye not that
the unrighteous shall not inherit the kingdom of
God? Be not deceived . . ." (1 Corinthians 6:9).
Again, we are admonished, "Let no man deceive
you with vain words; for because of these things
cometh the wrath of God upon the sons of disobedience" (Ephesians 5:6).

The one who is truly born of God does not
live a life of sinning. The one practicing righteousness is righteous; and that righteousness

stems from the new nature within. It could not be the fruit of the old nature. The practice of righteousness does not make a man holy in the sight of God; but because man is made righteous by the work of Christ, as revealed in the gospel and received by faith, his life will be one that practices righteousness. No works of the law, no striving of the flesh, no self-laboring will ever cause a man to be declared righteous in the sight of a holy God. This principle was stated clearly by Paul,

> Knowing that a man is not justified by the works of the law, but by the faith of Jesus Christ, even we have believed in Jesus Christ, that we might be justified by the faith of Christ, and not by the works of the law; for by the works of the law shall no flesh be justified (Galatians 2:16).

Simple faith in the righteous One, the Lord Jesus Christ, results in His righteousness being imputed to us by God. And His holiness dwelling within becomes the *source* of the believer's practice of righteousness.

Likewise, Satan is the source for the practice of sin. Verse 8 states it clearly, "He that committeth [practices] sin is of the devil. . . ." Even as God is the wellspring from which righteousness comes, so the devil is the fountain from which sin comes. The verse continues, "For the devil sinneth from the beginning."

We can then be certain of two things, as stated in these verses. First, the person made righteous by Christ acts righteously; second, the person practicing sin has the devil as his instigator. Sin has a diabolical character. Moral conflict in humanity is not associated with mere ideas, but with Satan. Man's affiliation with the devil is described in Ephesians 2:2.

John Gill has written: "He who makes sin his constant business, and the employment of his life, whose life is a continued series of sinning, he is of the devil. Being like him, their father, doing his lusts, living continually in sin as he does, they resemble him, as children do their parents."

The contrast presented in these verses is unmistakable. Living righteously is a proof of being born of God; doing evil speaks of the devil's fatherhood. Again, we must be reminded that the Greek verb "do" is in the present tense and emphasizes continuous action. The one who lives a holy life is marked as a Christian. Remember, his good works do not make him a Christian, but he practices righteousness because he *is* a Christian. In contrast is the one who practices sin. Its origin is the devil. Significantly, the Bible never says this of a person who has received the Savior. Two parentages are in contrast. As children of God, we possess the characteristic not to sin; on the other hand, Satan's children sin always.

THE MAIN CHARACTERISTIC (v. 9)
What a shocker this verse is! It has often been used as a proof of "sinless perfection." But it must be read in the light of the preceding verse and in the context of the apostle's full development of his theme.

The absolute statement, "Whosoever is born of God doth not commit sin" (v. 9), does not apply only to a certain class of Christians. It is true of *every* believer, everyone who is begotten of God. This therefore may be said without exception of every person who has been born from above by the Spirit of God.

Consider, please, what this verse does *not* say. It does not say that a person who is born of God never commits an occasional act of sin, but he does not make it his trade or practice, the course of his life. Again the verb "commit" is in the present tense, indicating continuous action. J. N. Darby translates this verse, "Whosoever has been begotten of God does not practice sin." This in no way conflicts with John's previous statement, "If we say that we have no sin, we deceive ourselves, and the truth is not in us" (1 John 1:8). There is a difference between *having* sin and *doing* sin.

Here is the question: Why does the believer not practice sin? John says it is because "His seed remaineth in him, and he cannot sin, because he is born of God." The new nature dwells in every Christian. Some translations capitalize the word "His," implying that it is God's seed that remains in the believer. This seed is the new nature, the new man formed within the soul at salvation. That which is born of God in the believer, the new man, cannot sin. God's seed abides within the believer; it cannot become defective.

I wonder if something else might be true here also? In 1 Peter 1:23 we read, "Being born again, not of corruptible seed, but of incorruptible, by the word of God, which liveth and abideth forever." The same truth is declared by James, "Of His own will begot He us with the word of truth . . ." (James 1:18). The Lord Jesus Himself described the character of those who do not believe on Him: "And ye have not His word abiding in you" (John 5:38). This is the engrafted word by which we have been made partakers of the divine nature (James 1:21). Nothing grows out of a carrot seed except a carrot; an apple seed brings forth an apple tree. So James inquires, "Can the fig tree, my brethren, bear olive berries? Either a vine, figs? So can no fountain yield both salt water and fresh" (James 3:12). Because God's seed remains in the believer, it is impossible for a true Christian to *practice* sin. He no longer desires it. To live a wicked life, therefore, is foreign to true conversion.

Now, I am not ignoring the fact that the old nature is still within the believer. "That which is born of the flesh is flesh" (John 3:6). Nor am I denying that "the carnal mind is enmity against God" (Romans 8:7). This *old* nature is sinful, and it can produce nothing else. But the *new* nature is of the Lord, for we are "partakers of the divine nature." It is as incapable of sin as God is. When the Christian recognizes that he has a dual nature—one of sin and the other of God—he will be able to face life realistically. He will not want to dishonor his Heavenly Father by allowing anything to remain in his life that does not proceed from the new life. When on occasion the old nature asserts itself, and the believer lapses and allows an act of sin by thought, word, or deed, he can immediately do as 1 John 1:9 instructs, "If we confess our sins, He is faithful and just to forgive us our sins, and to cleanse us from all unrighteousness."

1 John 4:1-6

Beloved, believe not every spirit, but test the spirits whether they are of God; because many false prophets are gone out into the world.

By this know ye the Spirit of God: every spirit that confesseth that Jesus Christ is come in the flesh is of God;

And every spirit that confesseth not that Jesus Christ is come in the flesh is not of God; and this is that spirit of antichrist, of which ye have heard that it should come, and even now already is it in the world.

Ye are of God, little children, and have overcome them, because greater is He that is in you, than he that is in the world.

They are of the world; therefore speak they of the world, and the world heareth them.

We are of God. He that knoweth God heareth us; he that is not of God heareth not us. By this know we the spirit of truth, and the spirit of error.

10

How to Spot the Devil's Kids

Federal law is now calling for "truth in advertising." The labels of products must contain an accurate listing of the ingredients. The consumer is encouraged to "read carefully before using." A similar caution is given to believers in 1 John 4:1-6. Before a believer swallows all that is packaged "Christian," he is advised to do some testing. Not everyone who comes in the name of Christ is a representative of the truth. The apostle Peter warned,

But there were false prophets also among the people, even as there shall be false teachers among you, who secretly shall bring in destructive heresies, even denying the Lord that bought them, and bring upon themselves swift destruction.

And many shall follow their pernicious ways, by reason of whom the way of truth shall be evil spoken of (2 Peter 2:1,2).

The apostle John concluded the third chapter of

his epistle by referring to two important qualities of the Christian life: faith and love (v. 23). These two subjects form the content of chapter 4. The epistles always maintain a beautiful balance between belief and behavior, doctrine and life. The first concern of this passage is belief.

Beloved, believe not every spirit, but test the spirits whether they are of God; because many false prophets are gone out into the world (1 John 4:1).

Religious deceivers most certainly abound today! They have invaded our pulpits, our colleges, our theological seminaries, and even our homes. The false prophets of our day, sometimes masked in religious respectability, launch continual assaults upon God's Word and His Christ.

While changing planes at the Dallas-Fort Worth terminal, I was confronted by two young men who offered me a large, clothbound book. I asked them, "What do you believe about Jesus Christ?" Their evasive answers immediately raised questions in my mind about their belief. Further conversation revealed that they were of "that spirit of antichrist."

After John commanded us to "test the spirits," he presented a rule by which we can judge whether one is of God or not. He wrote,

And He is the propitiation for our sins, and not for ours only, but also for the sins of the whole world.

And by this we do know that we know Him, *if we keep His commandments* (1 John 2:2,3).

The relationship every teaching bears to the person and work of the Lord Jesus Christ determines whether or not it is of God. John's rule is actually twofold. First, there must be the confession that Jesus Christ came in the flesh; second, there must be a willingness to accept the doctrine of the apostles, which was inspired by God (1 John 4:6).

The belief that Christ came "in the flesh"—in actual physical and perfect humanity—involves not only His birth at Bethlehem but also His atoning death and resurrection. He had to become man so that He could die as our sin offering. He had to be raised from the dead so that the stamp of God's approval upon His atonement could be seen by everyone. The resurrection testified that the claims of God's righteousness had all been met. The teachings that you and I are willing to accept must therefore honor Christ. If they exalt His name, recognize His divine nature, accept His atoning sacrifice upon the cross, and profess His resurrection from the grave, they are true. But if they deny His incarnation and death for sin, they are of the spirit of antichrist—the very same spirit that will develop into the lawless one at the end of the age.

WHERE CHRIST IS REVEALED

The Bible contains the ultimate standard for truth. Christ is revealed within its pages, and all that we know of Him is found there. By saying this, however, we automatically confront the question of the inerrancy of Scripture. If the writers of the Bible claim freedom from error, then we must conclude that we have in these writings the ultimate standard for truth and a reliable criterion to "test the spirits." If they are not infallible, then we cannot trust any part of it, for it is not a revelation from God.

With full assurance we can say that the Bible is God's Book, and that it affirms its own truthfulness. We have much internal evidence. The Lord Jesus prayed, "Sanctify them through Thy truth; Thy word is truth" (John 17:17). David said in Psalm 19:7, "The law of the Lord is perfect. . . ." And we read in Psalm 119, "Thy word is true from the beginning, and every one of Thy righteous ordinances endureth forever" (Psalm 119:160). Because God's Word is perfect, sure, true, and eternal, we have this clear statement of Isaiah about those who deny it:

To the law and to the testimony; if they speak not according to this word, it is because *there is no light in them* (Isaiah 8:20).

And the apostle Paul wrote,

All Scripture is given by inspiration of God, and is profitable for doctrine, for reproof, for correction, for instruction in righteousness,

That the man of God may be perfect, thoroughly furnished unto all good works (2 Timothy 3:16,17).

The Bible was given to instruct us, guide us, exhort us, and to tell us what to believe. Every Christian must therefore give heed to this infallible Book.

HOW TO TEST THE SPIRITS

The apostle not only instructed his readers to

"test the spirits," rejecting all that is not of God, he also told them how. Three factors are important in judging the teaching of those who purport to present the Word of God.

First, if we are to "test the spirits" by the Word of God, we must know and hold fast to the truth contained in it. Paul wrote, "Prove all things; *hold fast* that which is good" (1 Thessalonians 5:21). He also said, *"Hold fast* the form of sound words, which thou hast heard of me, in faith and love which is in Christ Jesus" (2 Timothy 1:13). John warned, ". . . many false prophets are gone out into the world" (1 John 4:1).

A believer cannot afford to be careless about the Scriptures. If he does become lax, he certainly will not lose his eternal life because of it—but he may lose his reward. Revelation 3:11 warns, "Behold, I come quickly; *hold that fast* which thou hast, that no man take thy crown."

Second, false doctrine must be avoided and hated. Many Christians do not seem to feel it is important for them to consider whom or what they hear. But God thinks differently. The apostle Paul indicated this strongly, for he said that if anyone, including himself or an angel, did not preach the truth, he was to be rejected.

But though we, or an angel from heaven, preach any other gospel unto you than that which we have preached unto you, let him be accursed.

As we said before, so say I now again, If any man preach any other gospel unto you than that ye have received, let him be accursed (Galatians 1:8,9).

Well-meaning Christians have often said to me,

"I know the pastor of my church is really not preaching the Bible. But our family has belonged to that church for years, and I just don't feel I can leave it now." Friend, if that is your situation and attitude, *you are wrong!* You will have to answer for it at the *bema*, the judgment seat of Christ. If a man forsakes the wholesome words of Scripture and teaches contrary to sound doctrine, he is proud and foolish. He is *not* to be heard. According to 1 Timothy 6:4, he is "doting," which means "sick." His error is infectious, leading to destruction. No wonder John warned in his second epistle,

For many deceivers are entered into the world, who confess not that Jesus Christ cometh in the flesh. This is a deceiver and an antichrist.

Look to yourselves, that we lose not those things which we have wrought, but -that we receive a full reward.

Whosoever transgresseth, and abideth not in the doctrine of Christ, hath not God. He that abideth in the doctrine of Christ, he hath both the Father and the Son.

If there come any unto you, and bring not this doctrine, receive him not into your house, neither bid him Godspeed;

For he that biddeth him Godspeed is partaker of his evil deeds (2 John 7-11).

The unerring, final test of truth is the Bible. By God's Word we are born again (1 Peter 1:23). By God's Word we grow (1 Peter 2:2). By God's Word abiding in us, prayer is answered (John 15:7). If we are to be strong Christians, built up in the most holy faith, we must allow God's

Word to become operative in our lives (Acts 20:32). How important is the Bible! By it we must try the spirits.

THE APOSTLE'S APPEAL (v. 1)

Great tenderness and intensity are found in the appeal of the apostle John, "Beloved, believe not every spirit, but test the spirits. . . ." In our present age, experience is exalted above the Word of God. The Christian public is enamored by claims of healings, miracles, and signs. The child of God must therefore be very discerning. Remember, friend, while Moses and Aaron were working miracles in the land of Egypt, Jannes and Jambres were duplicating some of them. Remember too that Simon Magus imitated Philip. Satan is in the business of counterfeiting that he may deceive and mislead many, and we must be extremely careful not to be caught unawares.

The United States Secret Service detects and destroys approximately a half-million dollars in counterfeit bills and coins each year. The government has issued a booklet entitled "Know Your Money" to help spot bogus cash. If it is important to you and me to be able to detect counterfeit money, how much more important to be informed about spiritual phonies and false doctrines! We must apply the test to everyone, for Paul warned,

For such are false apostles, deceitful workers, transforming themselves into the apostles of Christ.

And no marvel; for Satan himself is transformed into an angel of light.

Therefore, it is no great thing if his ministers also be transformed as the ministers of righteousness, whose end shall be according to their works (2 Corinthians 11:13-15).

Tragically, the Christian public is gullible. They are easily deceived. Believers must "test the spirits," for "many deceivers are entered into the world, who confess not that Jesus Christ cometh in the flesh" (2 John 7).

THE ULTIMATE TEST (vv. 2,3)

Stated simply, the ultimate test of false teaching is this: "Every spirit that confesseth that Jesus Christ is come in the flesh is of God; and every spirit that confesseth not that Jesus Christ is come in the flesh is not of God" (vv.2,3). Wherever Satan is active, his efforts are directed to one purpose—to attack Christ. Christian, you must be certain to find out what a person believes about the Lord Jesus. Every doctrine, every teacher, every system of religion must be evaluated by this criterion. Our Lord's question to His disciples in Caesarea Philippi is still valid for today. "Who do men say that I, the Son of man, am?" (Matthew 16:13). Simon Peter's answer must be ours also: "Thou art the Christ, the Son of the living God." Anyone who denies that must be judged accordingly.

Every Christian has this responsibility, including you. I realize that you may be called "a heresy hunter," but you *must* examine the claims of religionists and make a clear judgment based upon the Word of God. As already stated, it contains the standard of all doctrine, and every believer without exception must evaluate what he hears. To do this effectively, you must read and search the Scriptures. You will then be able to determine whether a teaching is from the Spirit of God or not. You see, the Holy Spirit never speaks contrary to His Word. God's revelation is true, and it is the revelation of His Son, Jesus Christ. The reason you must make the examination and apply the test is stated in these words: "Because many false prophets are gone out into the world."

Christ must be proclaimed before men! A conflict rages all around us. The Spirit of God is at work in the world. But in opposition to Him is the spirit of antichrist, the "mystery of iniquity" already at work upon the earth. Believers must be ready to confess Christ in a world that is at enmity with Him. If the church becomes popular with the world, something is terribly wrong. Our Lord cautioned His disciples,

If ye were of the world, the world would love its own; but because ye are not of the world, but I have chosen you out of the world, therefore the world hateth you (John 15:19).

THE OUTCOME (vv. 4-6)
Though we will be hated by the world even while we are bearing witness to it, we have the assurance that we "have overcome them, because greater is He that is in you, than he that is in the world" (v. 4). The apostle does not hold the erroneous idea, nor does the Word of God teach it, that the world is gradually being leavened by the truth. It is not getting better

and better, soon to reach a state of righteousness. John made a sharp contrast when he
said, "*They* are of the world. . . . *We* are of
God" (vv. 5,6). The world hears the false
teachers because they say what it wants to hear.
John says that those who know God will accept
his message. On one hand, this was a claim to
divine inspiration, which rightfully belonged to
the apostle. Yet his words are certainly applicable today to those who are of God and hear His
Word. And that Word is to be the final judge of
all doctrine, teachers, and systems of religion.

In contrast is the one who is "not of God."
This person has never experienced the new
birth. He has been born into the world and he is
of the world. He is blind to the truth because he
has never been regenerated by the Spirit of
God. He is not enlightened to grasp that which
is from above. Therefore he rejects what is
divinely inspired. He is the natural man, unregenerate and unable to understand God's
revelation.

But the natural man receiveth not the
things of the Spirit of God; for they are
foolishness unto him, neither can he know
them, because they are spiritually discerned
(1 Corinthians 2:14).

When the believer obeys the warning of John
and tests what he hears, he is given this
promise: "By this *know* we the spirit of truth,
and the spirit of error" (v. 6). Every Christian is
promised the discernment to distinguish one
from the other. Because he is indwelt by the
Holy Spirit, the believer recognizes and
confesses the person and work of Jesus Christ.

This comes as he accepts and appropriates the "living and powerful" Word of God. The Savior's promise is true:

> But when the Comforter is come, whom I will send unto you from the Father, even the Spirit of truth, who proceedeth from the Father, He shall testify of Me;
>
> And ye also shall bear witness . . . (John 15:26,27).

The beloved Louis Talbot wrote in his book *Heresies Exposed*, "The days in which you and I are living are days in which Christians need to know their Bibles, for the only way by which we may know whether or not a system of teaching is of God is by viewing the system through the lens of Holy Writ—reading the system in the light of the Bible and not reading the Bible in the light of the system."

This is how you may spot the devil's kids!

1 John 4:7-11; 5:1,2

Beloved, let us love one another; for love is of God, and everyone that loveth is born of God, and knoweth God.

He that loveth not knoweth not God; for God is love.

In this was manifested the love of God toward us, that God sent His only begotten Son into the world, that we might live through Him.

Herein is love, not that we loved God, but that He loved us, and sent His Son to be the propitiation for our sins.

Beloved, if God so loved us, we ought also to love one another.

Whosoever believeth that Jesus is the Christ is born of God; and everyone that loveth Him that begot loveth him also that is begotten of Him.

By this we know that we love the children of God, when we love God, and keep His commandments.

11

Brotherly Love – a Necessity

John had been emphasizing that every Christian should have a mental keenness for right doctrine and a sensitive heart to discern false teaching. But he also knew human nature. He was aware that those who have a sharp eye on matters of belief are sometimes harsh and intolerant with those whose doctrines may be slightly different. Once again, a wonderful balance is presented in Scripture. The apostle warned strongly that doctrinal exactness must never be allowed to excuse a lack of love for any fellow believer.

Therefore, inspired by the Holy Spirit, John returned to one of the dominant themes of the epistle. He had stated it clearly in chapter 3:

And whatever we ask, we receive of Him, because we keep His commandments, and do those things that are pleasing in His sight.

And this is His commandment, that we

should believe on the name of His Son, Jesus Christ, and love one another, as He gave us commandment (1 John 3:22,23).

Just exactly what was that commandment? Our Lord expressed it as follows: "A new commandment I give unto you, that ye love one another; as I have loved you, that ye also love one another. By this shall all men know that ye are My disciples, if ye have love one to another" (John 13:34,35).

This day in which we live, with its complex problems and intense pressures, is no time to hedge on the matter of loving our fellow Christians. As followers of the Lord Jesus, we are in the family. We are related by the new birth. We are indwelt by the same Holy Spirit. We call upon the same Heavenly Father. And we comprise the "household of faith." As children of God's family, we possess the nature of our Heavenly Father—and that nature is love.

A LOVING GOD (vv. 7,8)

Before we can feel and express love, we must have a nature that loves. The Bible says, "God is love." It's part of His nature. Back in 1 John 1:5, John told us that God is light. The Lord's first recorded manifestation and words were in connection with light. "And God said, Let there be light: and there was light" (Genesis 1:3). But note, He never said, "Let there be love, and there was love," for love is His nature. It can only be *communicated*, it cannot be *created*. It is expressed by self-sacrifice. It is unbought, unsought, unconditional, and undeserved. Such is the love of God!

Love is the expression of the Divine personality that corresponds to His nature. It is "of God"; that is, it flows from God. This is a love determined by the character of the One who loves, for "God is love" (1 John 4:8). The only person who can love as God loves is the one who is born of Him. As believers in Christ, we have been made partakers of the Divine nature. Therefore, our affections will exhibit His nature. God is the origin of true Christian love. He is its author. We are both the reason and the model for His love.

William Marshall included these words in his book *Intercepted Letters:* "Love, in the Christian sense, is not a loose and boneless sentimentality. It involves mind and will, and is seen in the deliberate resolve to do others good regardless of our feelings toward them or theirs toward us. It is like the good will of God in sending Christ. . . . Love is in the right direction of the will. To love is to promote the highest interests of others, and to do what we can, under God, to make them sensible of God's purpose for them."

Every member of God's family is to manifest this love. And how are we to do that? As God did. But how has God's love shown itself? The apostle anticipated this question, and gives us the answer.

GOD'S LOVE MADE MANIFEST (vv. 9, 10)
John began verse 9 by saying, *"In this* was manifested the love of God toward us." The words "in this" mean literally, "in *our* case." The apostle is not speaking here of God's

general love to all of His creatures. Certainly, we recognize that He has shown His love in creating, in supporting, and in caring for His creation. But this refers to God's special love toward His own. And the passage tells us it has been shown in two ways: to bring us life, and to pay for our sins.

The first expression of *how* God loved us is found in the clause, "That we might live through Him." Love not only gives, it *sends*. God *sent* His Son that we might be rescued from spiritual death. In fact, the Greek scholar Vincent pointed out in *Word Studies in the New Testament* that John most often described the incarnation as a *sending*.

The apostle used the perfect tense in this verse, saying literally, "God *has sent* His only begotten Son." This underscores the fact that the results of God's sending are permanent. The offer and promise of salvation will not be withdrawn. No other act on God's part could so demonstrate His love as this amazing fact. Think of it! The very God against whom we have sinned, the God who is able either to save or to destroy, this God has sent His Son to be our Savior.

Christ came that you and I who were spiritually dead in trespasses and sins might be made alive by faith in Him. Paul wrote, "God commendeth His love toward us in that, *while we were yet sinners*, Christ died for us" (Romans 5:8). He said as well, "For we ourselves also were once foolish, disobedient, deceived, serving various lusts and pleasures, living in malice, and envy, hateful, and hating one another"

(Titus 3:3). God loved us while we were altogether unlovely. This quality of love was determined by the character of the One who loves—God Himself.

The second way God expressed His love was in atoning for our sins. "He loved us, and sent His Son to be the propitiation for our sins" (1 John 4:10). He manifested His love in sending His Son to this earth to suffer, to die, to be buried, and to be raised from the dead. This took care of two crucial problems for mankind. The first is the sin nature, which renders us dead. We are spiritually alienated from God; we are "dead" toward Him. The second is our conduct, which is totally unacceptable to God. God sent His Son "that we might have life." He came to be the "propitiation for our sins." The word "propitiation" comes from a Latin term which means, "that which renders one favorably disposed toward another." The death of Christ is the grounds whereby God is willing to act on the sinner's behalf.

How can God look with favor upon us? We displease Him by our conduct; we fail to meet His holy standards; we fall short of the mark. Because Christ took our place on the cross, bore our penalty, and was "wounded for our transgressions," the believer can now say with utmost confidence, "There is, therefore, now *no condemnation* to them who are in Christ Jesus" (Romans 8:1). What a manifestation of love! God sent His Son, the spotless Lamb, to bear our sins in His own body on the tree. The only One who never sinned was made sin for us. If that isn't love, what is?

Because He is holy in nature, God cannot treat sin lightly. To do less than punish sin and exact its penalty would be to make Him less than God. If the sinful soul is to have "life through Him," then something must be done with the sins which bar me from entering that life. What is the answer? God has judged and punished sin—but praise God, that judgment did not fall upon us. He poured it upon the person of our Substitute, the Lord Jesus Christ. "He sent Him to be the propitiation." Oh, what love! The hymnwriter said,

> A monument of grace,
> A sinner saved by blood,
> The streams of love I trace,
> Up to the fountain, God;
> And in His sovereign counsels see
> Eternal thoughts of love to me.

OUR RESPONSE TO GOD'S LOVE (v. 11)

God has shown His love by giving according to our need. Absolutely nothing in us merited the love of God that sent His Son into the world. As the songwriter has put it, "He loved me ere I knew Him, He drew me with the cords of love, and thus He bound me to Him." Our Lord said to His disciples, "Ye have not chosen Me, but I have chosen you . . ." (John 15:16).

The love of God in Christ came to us even before there was any spiritual movement toward Him on our part. Romans 5 says that it was "when we were yet *without strength*," "while we were yet *sinners*," and "when we were *enemies*" that God commended His love toward us. We must have a nature born from above to understand His wondrous love. John wrote, ". . . for love is of God, and everyone that loveth is born of God, and knoweth God" (1 John 4:7). Only as we are made partakers of the divine nature can we begin to love the God of love. We read in verse 16 of 1 John 4, "And we have known and believed the love that God hath to us."

The plea of the apostle John is simply this: "Beloved, if God so loved us, we ought also to *love one another*" (v. 11). This expresses the reason we should love. Because we have become partakers of the very nature of God, we ought to love one another. Someone has suggested that God's love is perfected (or "made complete") *toward* us as *sinners* (vv. 9, 10), and His love is also made complete *in* us as *sons* (v. 12).

Notice that the apostle used that little word "ought" in verse 11, ". . . ought also to love one another." That term expresses a special, personal obligation. We have been put into debt. God's love for us, unlovely as we are, has put us under the obligation to love one another. Yet His love operates *through* us to our fellowmen. Malachi Taylor said, "It [God's love] is a large treasure house to draw from. Every brother ought to feel safe with another brother because he is of God, knowing that this large love will be exercised toward him."

Christians are mirrors of the love of God. We bear witness of Him to the world just as Christ did. We are in Him; therefore, His love is the kind of love we have. Read again verses 14 through 16 of 1 John 4. Is God's love being demonstrated through each of us? Ask yourself, what has been my response to it?

BROTHERLY LOVE, IT MUST BE!

John had expressed the need for love among the brethren earlier in the epistle.

> In this the children of God are manifest, and the children of the devil: whosoever doeth not righteousness is not of God, neither he that loveth not his brother.
>
> We know that we have passed from death unto life, because we love the brethren. He that loveth not his brother abideth in death (1 John 3:10, 14).

John reiterates this truth here at the close of chapter four. But he strikes the anvil with even greater force, for he declares,

> If a man says, I love God, and hateth his brother, he is a liar; for he that loveth not his brother, whom he hath seen, how can he love God, whom he hath not seen?
>
> And this commandment have we from Him, that he who loveth God love his brother also (1 John 4:20, 21).

Let me quote a paragraph from J. C. Metcalfe in *The Overcomer:*

> There is much more that can be said about this link between the birth from above and the resultant entry into a completely new attitude, in which love is the predominant feature. The general life of the evangelical section of the church is a strange commentary on all this. The bitterness, strife, criticism, petty rivalry, and discourtesy which we so often meet raise the question as to the validity of our claims, and the value of those religious qualities and practices we consider to be so important. Do not

Paul's pungent words in the first three verses of 1 Corinthians 13 need to be read again and again, and rigidly and honestly applied in our own lives? Experiences, gifts, soundness of knowledge, and ministry, faith, charity, and even supreme sacrifice are swept aside, and love is enthroned alone.

What practical effects this love has upon every relationship of the believer within the family of God! If we truly love *God* and keep His commandments, then we will love the *children of God*. Paul's command to the Romans is unavoidable. "Wherefore, receive ye one another, as Christ also received us to the glory of God" (Romans 15:7). What a rebuke to our petty prejudices! How devastating to our excuses for mistreating our brethren in Christ! To claim a love for God and at the same time to reject, despise, and mistreat those who are brethren in the same family is totally incongruous.

A striking example of the operation of love for the brethren is found in the experience of the early church at Jerusalem. In one Spirit the believers in Jerusalem had been baptized into one body. Subsequently, Simon Peter was sent by God to a Gentile household in Caesarea. Accompanying him were some believing Jews from Jerusalem, and they were astonished that the Gentiles had also received the Holy Spirit. The apostles and brethren that were in Judea had heard what happened in the household of one who was not a Jew.

Peter was summoned to Jerusalem to explain why he had gone into the home of a "Gentile dog." You see, these Jewish Christians were filled with prejudice, and this was inexcusable, for they had experienced the love of God in Christ. Peter concluded his report to them with these words, "Forasmuch, then, as God gave them the same gift as He did unto us, who believed on the Lord Jesus Christ, what was I, that I could withstand God?" (Acts 11:17). The love of God in those Christians at Jerusalem then manifested itself in brotherly love for the new members of God's family who were Gentiles. This was the response: "When they heard these things, they held their peace, and glorified God, saying, Then hath God also to the Gentiles granted repentance unto life" (v. 18).

I can partially understand why those Jewish believers were at first unwilling to accept as brethren the Gentiles in Caesarea, even though their reluctance was inexcusable. But for the believers this side of Calvary, the open tomb, and Pentecost, to refuse to accept in Christian love others who know the same Savior, who have been regenerated by the same Holy Spirit, and who are members of the same body, is to disobey the commandment of our Lord. It causes us to question seriously their love for God.

"We love Him, because He first loved us" (1 John 4:19). What else can we do? Romans 5:5 declares, "The love of God is shed abroad in our hearts by the Holy Spirit who is given unto us." We also read, "The love of Christ constraineth us" (2 Corinthians 5:14). Love for fellow believers is the evidence of a true love for God. Remember, they are *in the family*. Mark it well!

This love is to be active toward *all* who are of the household of faith. They may be agreeable or disagreeable, but the reason for loving them is that they are born of God. "Everyone that loveth Him that begot loveth him also that is begotten of Him" (1 John 5:1). The new nature, possessing divine love, has a fellowship with God and with all who know Him.

For this is the love of God, that we keep His commandments: and His commandments are not burdensome (1 John 5:3).

Brotherly love—it *MUST BE!*

1 John 5:1-8

Whosoever believeth that Jesus is the Christ is born of God; and everyone that loveth Him that begot loveth him also that is begotten of Him.

By this we know that we love the children of God, when we love God, and keep His commandments.

For this is the love of God, that we keep His commandments: and His commandments are not burdensome.

For whatever is born of God overcometh the world; and this is the victory that overcometh the world, even our faith.

Who is he that overcometh the world, but he that believeth that Jesus is the Son of God?

This is He that came by water and blood, even Jesus Christ; not by water only, but by water and blood. And it is the Spirit that beareth witness, because the Spirit is truth.

For there are three that bear record in heaven, the Father, the Word, and the Holy Spirit; and these three are one.

And there are three that bear witness in earth, the Spirit, and the water, and the blood; and these three agree in one.

12

Conquerors in Christ

The apostle John did not waste time writing a lot of sentimental drivel about love. He made it clear that for the believer, the demonstration of love is simply the outworking of the new nature. First, God has loved us. Second, we love Him because He first loved us. Third, John added this plea: "Beloved, if God so loved us, we ought also to love one another" (1 John 4:11). That's the pattern God sets!

A VITAL RELATIONSHIP (vv. 1-3)
The apostle began by saying, "Whosoever believeth that Jesus is the Christ is born of God." Before a person can truly love God and keep His commandments, he must have the new nature. One must first be begotten of God, be born from above. The starting point is salvation.

Just what did the apostle mean when he said, "Whosoever believeth that Jesus is the Christ"?

He was calling for true faith in the Lord—not mere orthodox belief. This is the primary principle of the new birth, and it is entirely harmonious with all of Scripture on the subject. Philip told the Ethiopian eunuch, "If thou believest with all thine heart, thou mayest. And he answered and said, I believe that Jesus Christ is the Son of God" (Acts 8:37).

All who are begotten of God have come to know His purpose for sending the Lord Jesus. They believe the Father's revelation that He is truly the anointed One. He was charged with the responsibility of purchasing our redemption, and He was raised from the dead after accomplishing the work God gave Him to do. Believing that Jesus is the Christ begins at Bethlehem and carries on through to Calvary, the open tomb, and His return to the right hand of God. John in his gospel stated that all who accept these truths are "born, not of blood, nor of the will of the flesh, nor of the will of man, but of God" (John 1:13).

The natural outcome of the new birth is spelled out in 1 John 5:1, "Everyone that loveth Him that begot loveth him also that is begotten of Him." To love the Father is to love all who are His children. This principle was already discussed in 1 John 4. Love for our fellow Christians is the evidence of true love for God. But how can we know our love for the brethren is genuine? The foolproof test is a love for God *that keeps His commandments.* Unlike the decalog, these moral requirements are addressed to the new nature. They are not "burdensome"—not harsh and wearying. The ten commandments were addressed to the flesh and were oppressive. In fact, Peter made this plea to the council at Jerusalem: "Now, therefore, why put God to the test, to put a yoke upon the neck of the disciples, which neither our fathers nor we were able to bear?" (Acts 15:10). But it is not a burden for the new nature to respond to the love of God and keep His commandments.

Several adults expressed their pity for a little girl who was carrying a heavy baby. She exclaimed brightly, "Oh, but he is my brother!" For the one who has been begotten of God, the commandments of the Lord Jesus are not an odious duty but a delightful privilege. Christ said, "For My yoke is easy, and My burden is light" (Matthew 11:30).

A vital relationship with God through Jesus Christ results in love to the Father and in keeping His commandments. The spirit of obedience brings the entire life into subjection to Him. True brotherly love extends to all the children of God, within the realm of His commandments. The Lord Jesus said in John 14, "If ye love Me, keep My commandments. If a man love Me, he will keep My words . . ." (vv. 15,23).

A VICTORIOUS FAITH (vv. 4,5)

Peter told us how we are born from above. "Being born again, not of corruptible seed, but of incorruptible, *by the word of God*, which liveth and abideth forever" (1 Peter 1:23). This word is received by faith. "For by grace are ye saved through faith; and that not of yourselves, it is the gift of God—not of works, lest any man should boast" (Ephesians 2:8,9). Whether you think the phrase "it is the gift of God" refers to salvation or to the faith, one thing is certain: the grace, the salvation, the faith—all of these are *not* of ourselves. "Faith cometh by hearing, and hearing *by the word of God.*" Refuse His Word and there is no faith; hear and believe it and "faith cometh."

What is faith? What is its central quality? The believer is justified entirely by grace. "Therefore, it is of faith, that it might be by grace . . ." (Romans 4:16). I think it is quite evident that when the Bible says "we are justified by faith" or "saved by faith," it implies the renunciation of all merit in ourselves. The saving power is not in our faith but in its object, Jesus Christ! The focus is entirely upon the One we believe in. We are not justified by our faith, but because the demands of God's holiness have been satisfied. Christ met those demands by His sinless life and by bearing our sins in His body on the tree. Faith simply relies upon His work as satisfactory and complete. The believing sinner is satisfied with that which satisfied God—the work of His beloved Son.

The redemptive work of Christ on our behalf is received by faith. This puts us in the place of conquerors. "For whatever is born of God *overcometh* the world; and this is the victory that overcometh the world, *even our faith*" (1 John 5:4). Mark it well, friend! Our overcoming power is not in faith, but in the object of that faith, Jesus, the Son of God.

The triumphant Christian knows the triumphant Christ. He alone has been victorious over the world. Tell me, Christian friend, are you any match for the world? Indeed not! But you may sing with the poet,

> My faith has found a resting place,
> Not in device nor creed;
> I trust the Everliving One,
> His wounds for me shall plead.

Christ is not fighting the battle now that makes me a victor over the world. No indeed! He fought it and won it at the cross. He has died and is risen again. He is the victorious Christ!

The television coverage of a football bowl game in our city was blacked out, so I listened to portions of the game on the radio. But 3 hours after starting time, a telecast of the game was released for our viewing. The game had been videotaped, of course, and we were seeing a replay. I watched with some interest, but I had no doubt of the outcome. I had heard the final score on the radio. I had no need to guess who would win. I already knew. The contest had been completed! The same is true of the battle with Satan. It's already been won!

When the children of Israel were delivered from Egypt and their enemies, Moses cried, "I will sing unto the Lord, for He hath triumphed gloriously" (Exodus 15:1). So, every child of God may rejoice in the victory which Christ has wrought through His death and resurrection. All our victory is in Another. It does not come through *our* efforts but through *His* finished work. Our part is simply to believe.

The triumphant Christian is occupied with the Lord Jesus. He exults in the victory of the Savior. The object of our faith is Jesus the Christ. The warrant of our faith is the Bible, for in it we have the revelation of His Son. Are we overcomers? Yes we are! Here is the promise of our Lord, "These things I have spoken unto you, that in Me ye might have peace. In the world ye shall have tribulation: but be of good cheer; I have overcome the world" (John 16:33).

As children of God, we are *in* this world, but we are not *of* it. This world did not know Christ, and it does not know us. We are continually faced with opposition by the world system, which has its own god. It hates the true God and would impede our obedience to Him. But the believer, the one born of God, overcomes the world. What is the victory that overcomes the world? "Even our faith." Our trust is in the Son of God, and we obediently do His will. The conquering Savior assures our victory. What a great salvation!

A VINDICATING WITNESS (vv. 6-8)
The next portion of 1 John 5 is very difficult to interpret but is laden with blessed truth. As the apostle John by the Holy Spirit penned these words, his mind must have returned to his gospel, also written under the Spirit's inspiration. He had said, "But one of the soldiers, with a spear, pierced His [Jesus'] side, and immediately came there out blood and water. And he that saw it bore witness, and his witness is true; and he knoweth that he saith true, *that ye might believe*" (John 19:34,35). Remarkably, only John gives account of the pierced side of our Savior. He alone tells of the water and blood that came forth from His body. Water speaks of cleansing, blood speaks of expiation. We sing,

Let the water and the blood,
From Thy wounded side which flowed,
Be of sin the double cure,
Save from wrath and make me pure.

The guilty sinner is in desperate need of two great works: moral cleansing and release from guilt. Through the death of Christ, both propitiation and purification were accomplished, and they are given to all who receive Christ. The Holy Spirit is here on earth to bear record of that fact.

The history of Israel illustrates three facets of man's salvation: redemption, deliverance, and nearness to God. To rescue and save the chosen nation, Jehovah did three mighty deeds.

First, He redeemed them from death *in the land* of Egypt *by the blood*, and by the blood alone. God said, "When I see the blood, I will pass over you" (Exodus 12:13). By the death of the passover lamb, they were safe when the judgment came. Likewise, God justifies the ungodly, delivering them from spiritual death. Even though Israel was redeemed, however, they were still in the land of Egypt.

Second, God delivered His people out of the house of bondage and separated them unto Himself. He led them out by a pillar of fire and cloud. Passing through the Red Sea, they were "all baptized unto Moses in the cloud and in the sea" (1 Corinthians 10:2). They were delivered and separated from their enemies by water. The water destroyed their enemies and made them safe. This is beautifully pictured by baptism. It is a symbol of the work of Christ by which we are brought from darkness and death into newness of life.

Third, Israel was brought near to God, for He came down and dwelt among them. The shekinah, resting above the mercy seat and the ark of the covenant in the tabernacle, signified the presence of God in the the camp. Today, the Holy Spirit has been sent down by the ascended, glorified Christ to dwell corporately in the church (which is His body) and individually in the believer (whose body is the temple of the Holy Spirit).

These three vital elements, blood, water, and Spirit, are beautifully portrayed for us in the arrangement of the tabernacle and the temple. As a man entered the outer court, the first object he saw was the brazen altar. Within it was the consuming fire, speaking of divine justice. Blood was over the top of the altar for the eye of God, on the sides for the eye of the worshiper, and flowing around the base to indicate completeness. Remember, ". . . without shedding of blood is no remission" (Hebrews 9:22).

Beyond the brazen altar with its blood stood another vessel—the laver. It contained water which was applied to the hands and feet of the priests who served in the sanctuary. It spoke of cleansing from the daily, outward sins of life. The Israelite was justified from the guilt of sin by the blood; he was cleansed from the power and pollution of sin, just as we are by "the washing of water by the word" (Ephesians 5:26). Then the worshiper was prepared to enter the holy place and draw near to the location where God was abiding, the holy of holies.

This same remarkable order was also followed in the sacrifice of the red heifer in Numbers 19. That animal was to be killed outside the camp and burned, and the blood was to be sprinkled before the tabernacle. A person who was ceremonially clean would then take up the ashes and lay them in a clean place nearby. These ashes, mingled with water, were to be "kept for the congregation of the children of Israel for a water of *separation:* it is a purification for sin" (Numbers 19:9). In this rite we again see the twofold emblems of water and blood in their undivided application of redemption and separation.

The combination of water and blood was also present in the teaching and example of our blessed Savior. The night of His betrayal and arrest, He taught the same lesson to His disciples (see John 13). The text says, ". . . supper being ended" (v. 2). What supper was it? It was the *passover* supper, a picture of the blood of the Passover Lamb. "Christ, our passover, is sacrificed for us" (1 Corinthians 5:7).

After the supper was completed, He "took a towel, and girded Himself. After that He poureth water into a basin, and began to wash the disciples' feet" (John 13:4,5). This was the water. The Savior then proceeded to tell them *why* He was about to wash their feet. He had come from God, and He would soon return to God. He came to die, to shed His blood and redeem His people. He was about to go to the Father, to send forth His Spirit upon His own, and to make them fit for service by purifying them. Even now He is sitting at the right hand of the Father as our Advocate. He pleads our cause, maintains our fellowship with the Father, and gives us victory over the world and sin.

Redemption by blood is now completed. It has been accomplished once and for all. No more do we need to offer a sacrifice, but we do need the washing of our feet, the daily washing of water by the Word. Just as the blood redeemed the Israelites in the land of Egypt and the water delivered them out of that contamination, so the blood of Christ redeems and cleanses us and the water of the Word keeps us pure.

Someone has suggested that there are two great heresies in our day. With one it is all blood and no water; with the other it is all water and no blood. One says, "Since Jesus paid it all, it makes no difference how I live." The other says, "If I live right, I have no need of the blood." Neither is correct. The text says, "This is He that came by water and blood, even Jesus Christ; not by water only, but by water and blood" (1 John 5:6).

The blessed Holy Spirit Himself bears witness that this is true. He is here on this earth, indwelling the believer to bear witness to Christ and His work. His presence is the abiding witness that our redemption has been accomplished, and that God has accepted the work of His Son by His death and resurrection. "And there are three that bear witness in earth, the Spirit, and the water, and the blood; and these three agree in one" (1 John 5:8).

My friend, we have been discussing the secret of our victory. It begins with the right relationship with God. We must first be born again by receiving the Lord Jesus as personal Savior.

Next, we must acknowledge that our victory is in Christ. It was His obedience and sacrifice that satisfied God's wrath—not our own. Third, we have the Holy Spirit's witness of our triumph in Christ. Let us therefore walk in confidence and faith. Satan is overcome; we are conquerors in Christ!

1 John 5:16,17

If any man see his brother sin a sin which is not unto death, he shall ask, and He shall give him life for them that sin not unto death. There is a sin unto death; I do not say that he shall pray for it.

All unrighteousness is sin, and there is a sin not unto death.

13

Sin
Unto Death

Nothing is so moving or needful as the demonstration of love in the family. You and I have found it essential in our human relationships, and it is even more important among the children in the family of God. As a father, I have seen a tear trickle down the cheek of my little daughter when her sister was getting a spanking. When one child pleads with her father on behalf of another, it's an unforgettable moment. Could fellowship in the church be complete without this same mutual concern?

As members of God's family, we can freely ask anything of our Heavenly Father. Of course, His own will is uppermost in each case, just as earthly fathers have a desire for their children. And He is wiser than we are. We may make mistakes by asking Him for improper things; nevertheless, we are commanded to ask "anything according to His will." When we do, we can count on receiving what we ask. As an introduction to the verses under consideration, please read 1 John 5:14,15. Surely we would *not* want God to grant us anything that would be contrary to His will!

The apostle Paul issued this command: "Brethren, if a man be overtaken in a fault, ye who are spiritual restore such an one in the spirit of meekness, considering thyself, lest thou also be tempted" (Galatians 6:1). This harmonizes perfectly with our Lord's instructions to His disciples, "If I, then, your Lord and Master, have washed your feet, ye also ought to wash one another's feet" (John 13:14). Because we have concern for our children in the family, we ask the Father for His intervention on their behalf. "If any man see his brother sin a sin which is not unto death, he shall ask, and He shall give him life for them that sin not unto death" (1 John 5:16).

HOW GOD CHASTENS

We must recognize that not all sickness in the life of a believer is chastisement from God. Many earnest, godly, obedient Christians suffer illness and physical pain. God certainly is not chastening them! Indeed, He may actually be manifesting His own glory and strength through their weakened physical condition. If you are a suffering saint reading these words, I trust that you will clearly understand what I am saying. The Father may send affliction, not as punishment but as His way of promoting your spiritual growth and training. In Hebrews chapter 12, the author indicated four reasons why God chastens His children.

1. *As proof of our sonship* (Hebrews 12:6-8). The Heavenly Father does not trouble Himself about those who are not members of the family. But He has promised to guard and guide and conform to Himself all who bear His name. "He doth not afflict willingly" (Lamentations 3:33). Because we are His sons, however, He chastens us in love.

2. *In His right as Father* (v. 9). God is a perfect Father. He deals wisely and perfectly with His children. He knows all about us. He desires the very best for us and acts accordingly. Let us therefore "be in subjection unto the Father of spirits, and live."

3. *For our spiritual benefit* (v. 10). God is constantly working to conform us to the image of His Son so that we might partake of His holiness. The field must be plowed before it can yield a harvest. The fruit must be crushed before it can produce a sweet and satisfying juice. Likewise, trial and blessing are inseparably linked in God's economy.

4. *To bring forth fruit* (v. 11). When the obedient Christian endures adversity, his faith increases. The time of pruning must come. It's not a joyous time, but it results in new branches and fruit. Remember, friend, the gardener's hand is always near the plant he is pruning. As the Father's hand comes near to teach, chasten, and prune us, we shrink back from it. "Now no chastening for the present seemeth to be joyous, but grievous; nevertheless, afterward it yieldeth the peaceable fruit of righteousness unto them who are exercised by it."

When the believer continues to presume upon

the grace of God in order to justify some sin,
however, God's hand of chastening sometimes
comes in harsh severity—even "unto death."

THE "SIN UNTO DEATH" (1 John 5:16,17)

John wrote verses 16 and 17 to give us a dire
warning. Remember, the Christian is in no
danger of losing his eternal salvation. God in
His grace has saved him. He has delivered him
from spiritual death. "No condemnation" is the
promise for all who have been justified by the
grace of God. The apostle John is speaking here
to believers, and to believers only. They alone
are the possessors of eternal life.

Sometimes, however, a Christian allows the
old nature to take control. He presumes upon
the grace of God by practicing some sin that
brings dishonor to the name of Christ. When
that occurs, God must chasten the believer.
"For whom the Lord loveth He chasteneth, and
scourgeth every son whom He receiveth" (Hebrews 12:6). If the sinning believer does not respond to the loving, chastening hand of God, if
he is not "exercised by it," look out! God may
bring death—physical death. "There is a sin
unto death; I do not say that he shall pray for it"
(1 John 5:16).

Several facts about this "sin unto death"
should be noted: (1) The article "a" is not
present in the Greek text. The verse could
therefore be rendered, "there is sin unto
death." This suggests that John was probably
not speaking of one certain sin, but of the continuation of some sin. (2) The verb translated
"sin" in verse 16 is in the present tense, and

means "continually sinning." The sin unto death is therefore not a single, isolated act, but one that has been repeated over and over again by the disobedient child of God. (3) The words "if any man see" indicate that it is some overt action, probably affecting the entire assembly of believers. (4) It is definitely the sin of a brother. It is committed by a child of God and therefore concerns the family.

You may be hesitant to admit the possibility of such a sin and ask, "Would God really allow physical death as an extreme chastisement for sin in the life of one of His children?" The Scriptures themselves give the answer.

BIBLICAL EXAMPLES

That God in His mercy may bring death to a believer who continues in certain sins, thereby removing him from this earth, is demonstrated in both Old and New Testaments. For instance, 1 Kings 13 tells about an elderly prophet who was allowed to die because of his disobedience. Then, too, Korah and his followers usurped the office of the priesthood, deliberately rebelling against God's established order, and the earth "swallowed them up."

Ananias and Sapphira may also have committed the sin unto death (see Acts 5). In the early days of the church at Jerusalem, the believers shared willingly what they had. Many who owned lands and houses sold them and brought the proceeds to the apostles. Then, as the believers in that church had need, funds were distributed to them. Luke tells us that "great grace was upon them all" (Acts 4:33).

Ananias and his wife Sapphira also sold their
possessions, but they secretly decided to hold
back part of the money they had received in the
sale. Although it was their privilege to do so,
they pretended that they were giving the entire
amount to the church leaders. They therefore
lied to the Holy Spirit and committed a sin that
brought God's hand of judgment upon them.
He struck them dead in the presence of the
apostles. Remember, Ananias and Sapphira
were Christians, children of God. But the Lord
chastened them "unto death," taking them out
of the assembly and using them as an example
to the church.

Another vivid illustration of the "sin unto
death" is found in 1 Corinthians 11. The
believers in Corinth had made a mockery of the
Lord's Supper. They had brought it down to the
level of a common meal as observed by the Corinthians. In that assembly, the *agape* or love
feast was a meal of fellowship that preceded the
observance of the Lord's table. But its original
purpose had been grossly perverted. The leaven
of the old feasts of idolatry had corrupted the
memorial. The Corinthians were desecrating the
communion service. To them Paul delivered this
stern warning:

Wherefore, whosoever shall eat this bread,
and drink this cup of the Lord, unworthily,
shall be guilty of the body and blood of the
Lord.

But let a man examine himself, and so let
him eat of that bread, and drink of that cup.

For he that eateth and drinketh unworthily, eateth and drinketh judgment to

himself, not discerning the Lord's body
(1 Corinthians 11:27-29).

The Corinthians had turned the remembrance of
Christ's death into a worldly festival. They were
impatiently eating before the others could join
in. Some were hungry and others were drunk.
The crux of their wrong conduct is described in
the phrase, "not discerning the Lord's body."
They were participating "unworthily."

When a believer continues to sin, refusing to
confess and forsake it, he will be chastened by
the Lord. The Corinthians were guilty of unconfessed sin, and God's chastening took the
form of sickness and physical death. "For this
cause many are weak and sickly among you,
and many sleep" (1 Corinthians 11:30). (The
word "sleep" is used repeatedly in the New
Testament to indicate physical death.) Their
particular sin was the selfish and willful abuse of
the Lord's table. This, or any other unjudged
sin, may cause the believer to experience the
chastening hand of God—today as well as then.

A. T. Pierson once said, "It has been my habit
for years to spend the last half hour before I go
to sleep in looking over the day, asking God to
let me see where wood, hay, and stubble have
found incorporation in my life building. I would
ask Him to judge me then and there, and to
burn up the wood, hay, and stubble that
nothing may stand but gold, silver, and
precious stones." Good advice!

A THIRD EXAMPLE
Let me turn your attention to 1 Corinthians 5
which tells of another situation that occurred in

the church. The apostle Paul had received word that a case of flagrant immorality was going uncorrected. A man in that church had his father's wife; that is, his stepmother. Although we are not certain of the exact nature of this relationship, we do know that it was contrary to the will of God. The sinful conduct of this member of the congregation was now public information and was bringing reproach to the church.

The apostle insisted that the church take immediate action on the matter. They had not severed fellowship with him, nor had they asked God to remove the man from their assembly—by death if necessary. The Christians at Corinth were described as being "puffed up." Pride kept them from action. Paul therefore instructed them, "Deliver such an one unto Satan for the destruction of the flesh, that the spirit may be saved in the day of the Lord Jesus" (1 Corinthians 5:5). No call for the church to pray for this man! One thing was required—he should be removed. I believe he was committing a sin unto death.

Here is the critical question: Can such a man be restored to fellowship with God? In Paul's second letter to the Corinthians he urged the church to forgive this man and to comfort him. What had happened? No doubt he had heard the reading of the first epistle and had seen the wickedness of his sin. He realized that it had brought disgrace upon Christ and His church. Therefore, he had confessed and forsaken that sin, and had cried out to God in true repentance. Consequently we read,

SIN UNTO DEATH / 165

Sufficient to such a man is this punishment, which was inflicted by the many.

So that on the contrary ye ought rather to forgive him, and comfort him, lest perhaps such a one should be swallowed up with overmuch sorrow.

Wherefore, I beseech you that ye would confirm your love toward him (2 Corinthians 2:6-8).

This man's sin was decidedly worthy of God's judgment hand which would have resulted in death. But the disobedient believer had repented and turned from his sin. He had fled to the gracious, loving arms of the Heavenly Father, and the Father had spared him.

These words of the apostle Paul have deep significance: "Therefore, brethren, we are debtors, not to the flesh, to live after the flesh. For if ye live after the flesh, ye shall die; but if ye, through the Spirit, do mortify the deeds of the body, ye shall live" (Romans 8:12, 13).

Christian friend, if there is sin in your life, right now take the scriptural route and confess that sin. Forsake it, lest it break out in flagrant transgression, bring dishonor to the name of the Lord, and throttle the spiritual power of His church. At all cost avoid the risk of bringing upon yourself divine chastening that could lead, as it did in Corinth, to physical sickness or death. "As obedient children . . . be ye holy in all manner of life" (1 Peter 1:14, 15).

1 John 5:11-15, 18-21

And this is the record, that God hath given to us eternal life, and this life is in His Son.

He that hath the Son hath life; and he that hath not the Son of God hath not life.

These things have I written unto you that believe on the name of the Son of God, that ye may know that ye have eternal life, and that ye may believe on the name of the Son of God.

And this is the confidence that we have in Him, that, if we ask anything according to His will, He heareth us;

And if we know that He hear us, whatever we ask, we know that we have the petitions that we desired of Him.

We know that whosoever is born of God sinneth not, but he that is begotten of God keepeth himself, and that wicked one toucheth him not.

And we know that we are of God, and the whole world lieth in wickedness.

And we know that the Son of God is come, and hath given us an understanding, that we may know Him that is true; and we are in Him that is true, even in His Son Jesus Christ. This is the true God, and eternal life.

Little children, keep yourselves from idols. Amen.

14

Blessed Assurance!

"Call your witness," demanded the judge. The testimony of a sufficient number of creditable men of good character and report is always admitted in any case and in any court. The law of Moses called for the same procedure. In Israel, everything was proved and established by the honest reports of two or more people. Men were justified or condemned according to the proof established by their witness. If corroborating human testimony is acceptable, is not the witness of God even greater? "God is not a man, that He should lie" (Numbers 23:19). He can neither deceive nor be deceived. His word is true. He Himself has testified of the assurance of salvation and sure hope of Heaven for all who believe on His Son. There is no more certain witness!

A TWOFOLD WITNESS (vv. 9,10)
Carefully read these inspired words of John,

which tell of the testimony of God on our behalf:

> . . . for this is the witness of God which He hath testified of His Son.
>
> He that believeth on the Son of God hath the witness in himself; he that believeth not God hath made Him a liar, because he believeth not the record that God gave of His Son (1 John 5:9,10).

God's witness is twofold. His Word and His Spirit speak on our behalf. The *objective assurance* of the child of God rests upon the Bible. God has spoken! The apostle John said, "These things have I written unto you that believe on the name of the Son of God, that ye may know that ye have eternal life" (v. 13). We can stake our hope for eternity upon the Word of God!

We also have a *subjective assurance* from within. "The Spirit Himself beareth witness with our spirit, that we are the children of God" (Romans 8:16). When a Christian is willing to rest upon the witness of the Spirit in the Bible, he then receives the witness of the Spirit within his heart and mind. John said, "He that believeth on the Son of God hath the witness in himself" (v. 10). The Holy Spirit first leads the believer to a firm reliance upon the Scriptures, then He gives witness to the believer's spirit that he is indeed a child of God.

POSSIBILITY OF IGNORANCE

Those who have eternal life in the Son may be ignorant of the tremendous blessing of assurance. Therefore the apostle John said, "These things have I written unto you." The

Word, and the Word alone, gives believers the knowledge they need in order to know they are God's children. Blessed assurance for the child of God does *not* come by feeling or experience or other people's ideas. The Word brings that assurance! It tests our experience and our feeling and the doctrine of others. It alone is competent to do this. We have eternal life, and the Scriptures are written *that we may know it*.

The apostle John closed his epistle on a confident note. Again and again he wrote, "we know . . ." He set forth truths that every Christian should learn for himself. You and I must know with certainty that our sins have been forgiven, and that we have entered into a definite relationship with God through Jesus Christ.

Some Christians are filled with uncertainty. Others think it presumptuous to be so positive about their security in Christ. But if full assurance is not possible, then eternal life is but a scary chance. Several misconceptions are cleared away when we understand these truths.

1. *Assurance does not come through works.* We are not made the children of God by what we do. "For by grace are ye saved through faith; and that not of yourselves, it is the gift of God—*not of works*, lest any man should boast" (Ephesians 2:8,9). We are not saved by our own goodness, nor do we find assurance that way.

2. *Some lack assurance because they have never been born again.* Some people have had an emotional religious experience. Their habits of life may have changed dramatically. They have submitted to some religious ceremony like baptism. But Christianity is *life!* "By which are

given unto us exceedingly great and precious promises, that by these ye might be partakers of the divine nature . . ." (2 Peter 1:4). If a person does not possess the new life from above, received as a gift by accepting Jesus Christ, he will never be confident of his salvation.

3. *Others do not have assurance of eternal life because they do not believe what God says.* Sometimes people look within for a sense of security, rather than to the Word of God. They want to *feel* safe, when in reality they need simply to take God at His word. It's a matter of promise and trust, not just emotional feeling.

WHAT THE WORD TEACHES
Our focus is now directed to several important qualities every believer should possess as a member of God's family. They are:

Knowledge of eternal life (v. 13).
Knowledge of answered prayer (v. 15).
Knowledge of the new nature (v. 18).
Knowledge of our Father (v. 19).
Knowledge of God revealed in Christ (v. 20).

Certainly, "if any man be in Christ, he is a new creation; old things are passed away; behold, all things are become new" (2 Corinthians 5:17). This gives evidence of a *change* in life and desire. There is transformation! A new nature!

I read of a girl who lived in the highlands of Scotland and who had recently been converted. She came to church to recite the catechism, and to tell of her salvation. She floundered, blushed, and cried because she was unable to remember it. Finally she said in frustration, "I cannot explain it. It's like the washing of the sheep in yonder brook. Though I cannot tell where the water comes from or where it goes, I do know that when I take the sheep into the stream, the dirt is cleansed from the wool." Surely a change like she described, occurring in the believing sinners, brings a blessed assurance.

But the surest evidence of salvation is to have an unshaken confidence that is grounded upon the Word of God. "These things have I written," John said, "that ye may know that ye have eternal life." The psalmist cried, "Forever, O Lord, Thy word is settled in heaven" (Psalm 119:89). The apostle John added, "And this is the record, that God hath given to us eternal life, and this life is in His Son. He that hath the Son hath life; and he that hath not the Son of God hath not life" (1 John 5:11,12).

KNOWLEDGE THROUGH THE WORD (v. 20)
We come now to the final apostolic instruction from John. (The very last words of the Holy Spirit were also written by John and recorded in the book of Revelation.) This epistle is closed with a note of supreme confidence. "And we know that the Son of God is come." If I believe that Jesus—the rejected Jesus who was treated shamefully and crucified—if I believe that He was indeed the mighty Son of God, then I know that no event in the world's history compares with His incarnation.

Suppose I should question John and say, "How do we know He came?" I think he would take us to his gospel, where he had said, "But these are written, that ye might believe that Jesus is the Christ, the Son of God; and that

believing ye might have life through His name"
(John 20:31). At least seven great miracles are
recorded in the gospel of John. Each is a sign
that indelibly stamps Christ as the Son of God.
His words and His works *prove* that He is who
He said He was. Divine life, divine light, and
divine love have been manifested in Him. In
Christ's life and teaching we have the setting
forth of truth itself, and now "the Son of God is
come, and hath given *us* an understanding, that
we may know Him that is true" (1 John 5:20).

Not only do we have the full revelation of
God in the ministry of the Lord Jesus; we have
also seen God's light, we have partaken of
God's life, and we have experienced God's love.
God has given us understanding. We are born
of Him. We have received His Spirit. Once
again there is a blending of the Word and the
Spirit, the twofold witness. "He that believeth
on the Son of God hath the witness in himself"
(1 John 5:10). "And by this we know that He
abideth in us, by the Spirit whom He hath given
us" (1 John 3:24). Paul said in Galatians 4:6,
"And because ye are sons, God hath sent forth
the Spirit of His Son into your hearts, crying,
Abba, Father."

Friend, do you have assurance that you are a
child of God? Have you received the witness of
His Word concerning His Son? Have you
believed the Bible? Do you have the testimony
of His Spirit within? It is not necessarily emo-
tion or feeling, but the evidence of a new
relationship. It is the inward voice of God's
Spirit telling you that you are indeed the child

of God. If that is absent from your life, I urge you to give your heart to the Savior today.

ASSURANCE GIVES BOLDNESS (vv. 14, 15)
Christian assurance leads to boldness in prayer. The word "confidence" in verse 14 means "boldness" or "freedom of speech." As members of God's family, we are associated with the One from whom we can freely ask anything. There is but one condition: that we ask "according to His will." And we may be sure that, "He heareth us." Ours is the relationship of father and child. We have the immutable promise of endless blessings. No power can take them from us. God "hath blessed us with all spiritual blessings in heavenly places in Christ" (Ephesians 1:3). We have every reason to ask with believing prayer.

F. W. Grant has said, "We are down in the earth valleys too much, with our view bounded by objects which, however great to us, are small indeed in comparison with the immensity of the heavens. Let us get up where our blessings are. Let us seek to possess ourselves of these blessings. It is surely impossible that He who has made them our own should think of denying. If we are content to let the earth draw our boundary lines for us, and to limit ourselves by other things with which faith has no proper occupation, all will be as mean and beggarly in result as we have made ourselves mere beggars and not the children of God's family of faith." The assurance of our relationship with God gives us confidence when we pray.

FINALLY . . . (v. 21)

"Little children, keep yourselves from idols. Amen." What blessed assurance is ours as the children of God! We know the true God. We are in His Son, Jesus Christ. We are members of the divine family. Knowing Him, we should have no eye nor ear nor heart for any other object. An idol is anything and everything that draws the affection and devotion of the heart and soul away from the Lord Jesus Christ. What a tender plea from the apostle! "Little children, keep [guard] yourselves from idols."

Anything that creeps into the affections and usurps the decisions of the heart—that unique place that belongs to Him alone—is an idol. Dear fellow believer, let nothing of the world grip you and hold you and dominate you until your mind and thoughts are subject to it. May the Son of God, who has been made known to us and whom we know, be the center and circumference of our lives. May we say now, as restored Israel in a future time will say, "What have I to do anymore with idols? I have heard Him, and observed Him" (Hosea 14:8).

Let me ask you this pointed question: Are you *in the family*? Have you been born again by faith in Jesus Christ? There is no better time than now to make that decision. I plead with you to receive Him today.

If you are a Christian, what kind of family member are you? Do you have assurance? Is there joy within your heart? Are you pleasant to be with—part of the solution rather than part of the problem? Is everything all right between you and the Father? Or must you hang your head because of some cherished, unconfessed sin? Make things right today. Then you'll experience the full blessing of John's words:

> That which we have seen and heard declare we unto you, that ye also may have fellowship with us; and truly our fellowship is with the Father, and with His Son, Jesus Christ (1 John 1:3).